TIFFANY GREER

CAMPING COOKBOOK

Delicious and Easy Recipes for
Unforgettable Outdoor Dining Adventures
(2024 Beginner Guide)

First edition

This book was professionally typeset on Reedsy.
Find out more at reedsy.com

Contents

1

Introduction

When the experience of spending a night by the campfire is considered, a sense of nostalgia emerges, tied to the anticipation of crafting the perfect roasted marshmallow. Regrettably, after consecutive days of simple meals like hotdogs and no-fuss suppers, this cozy sensation seems to fade away. Throughout time, outdoor enthusiasts have developed various techniques for utilizing campfires to cook meals, with some being more intricate than others. For instance, while some hiking and camping trips might not demand the construction of a roasting spit (unless fueled by excessive enthusiasm), many strategies have been born from such scenarios.

The most uncomplicated method for campfire cooking employs direct heat. Two approaches exist for achieving this. The first, a traditional trick often employed by boy scouts, entails individually wrapping food items in aluminum foil before placing them on the hot, burning embers. While it demands consistent monitoring, this method is highly effective for dishes requiring high temperatures. The second approach involves situating a grill over an outdoor blaze and preparing food similarly to how one would in a backyard. Although this method produces less immediate heat, resulting in slightly longer cooking times, it remains viable.

For dishes like soups, stews, and pasta, the presence of pots and pans is indispensable. You simply need to establish a fire for cooking and let it transition to a bed of glowing coals before positioning the pot or pan over them. Skill in managing the quantity and intensity of these hot coals is key, as the heat can become volatile rather easily. The positive aspect is that, once mastered, cooking at the campsite parallels using a kitchen stove in terms of simplicity.

Camping differs somewhat from home cooking, as the luxury of ordering pizza is not readily available in case of mishaps. Therefore, when embarking on campsite cooking, investing a bit of effort into meal planning can yield substantial benefits. Not only will your recipes turn out better, but they will also be easier to execute. Pre-arrange each meal and snack prior to the camping trip to ensure that you don't deplete your food reserves or find yourself reluctantly consuming breakfast crisps on the initial night. The specifics of your plan will naturally vary depending on the nature of your camping expedition.

2

Necessary Items for Cooking While Camping

U ndoubtedly, savoring nourishing meals outdoors constitutes one of the most enjoyable aspects of camping. This endeavor need not be overly intricate;

rather, with some careful planning, creative thinking, and the essential tools, one can whip up exquisite dishes in the open air. While certain individuals might perceive camping as stressful and potentially taxing, especially concerning food provisions, it generally becomes simpler to prepare meals if your camping setup is as convenient as possible. To ensure the well-being of you and your companions, it's advised to avoid perishable foods and adhere rigorously to proper hygiene protocols.

1.1 Checklist of Essential Kitchen Items for Camping Crafting delectable outdoor meals isn't a daunting task with a bit of forethought, ingenuity, and the correct equipment. The joy of relishing excellent cuisine amid nature's beauty remains a prime attraction of camping. In a futuristic scenario, you might arrive at your camping spot equipped with a pre-planned menu, ready to kindle the flames and commence your culinary journey. Thereafter, you could indulge in your feast and unwind without a care.

1. **Camp Stove**

   A camp stove stands as a crucial gear piece if you intend to engage in cooking during your upcoming camping venture. Depending on your cooking requirements, you may opt for a single or dual burner, a cantilevered or table-top design. Safety remains paramount while cooking, necessitating prudent precautions. If you're camping in tents, a caravan, or a motorhome, it's imperative to avoid cooking within these enclosures due to potential fire hazards. Additionally, inadequate ventilation could lead to the accumulation of toxic carbon monoxide.

2. **Portable Cooler**

   For preserving food freshness, chilling milk, and keeping beverages cold, portable coolers are indispensable. Available in diverse shapes, sizes, and types, these coolers serve as a shield against spoilage. If packing space is at a premium, compact cool bags offer a space-efficient alternative.

3. **Camp Stove Fuel**

Owning a camp stove is futile without a reliable fuel source. Different stoves require specific types of fuel, but butane (typically in blue high-pressure cylinders) or propane (in red cylinders) are commonly used and safe options. Gas, being portable and safe, constitutes an excellent cooking fuel. It's recommended to review our guide on gas and liquid fuels before employing camping fuel.

4. **Dining Ware**

While seemingly obvious, it's easy to overlook the need for eating and drinking utensils. Opting for reusable dinnerware is not only eco-friendly but also preferable to single-use paper plates and disposable cutlery. The following items are necessary:

- Plates
- Bowls
- Cups
- Mugs
- Forks and knives
- Teaspoons and spoons
- Serving dishes

1. **Camp Cooking Pots and Pans**

Whether utilizing specialized camping cookware or improvising with home kitchen utensils, certain tools are essential for preparing meals. The market offers an array of pots and pans, with custom camping cookware generally excelling in lightweight design, durability, and portability. If planning to cook substantial quantities for a larger group, remember to carry larger utensils.

2. **Portable Camping Kettle**

Packing a kettle facilitates tea or coffee brewing, as well as preparing pasta or rice. Various camping kettle options exist, including aluminum and stainless steel models, along with collapsible folding kettles. For newcomers camping at sites with electricity, any kettle rated around 2kw or less is sufficient.

3. **Cooking Utensils**

Irrespective of the recipe, certain utensils like knives for slicing, wooden spoons for stirring, and spatulas for flipping are indispensable. The following items should be included:

- Wooden spoon
- Large spoons
- Tongs
- Spatula
- Whisk
- Sharp knife
- Chopping board

1. **Water Container**

A readily available water supply is a matter of convenience. Utilize a tap at your campsite to refill containers as needed. Foldable water containers with taps are purchasable at outdoor stores, providing a portable and easily storable solution.

2. **First Aid Kit**

Prioritizing safety is paramount when camping, necessitating a compact first aid kit. Burns and cuts are commonplace while cooking, making items like plasters and bandages invaluable. The kit should include:

- Various plasters
- Disposable sterile gloves
- Assorted bandages
- Tweezers
- Scissors
- Cleaning wipes
- Thermometer
- Adhesive tape
- Antiseptic cream
- Pain relievers

1. **Foldable Camping Toaster**

Toast serves as an affordable, fulfilling camping meal. Carrying a foldable camping toaster eliminates the need for transporting one from home. It's a convenient tool for toasting bread, breakfast sandwiches, teacakes, and even melting cheese on toast.

2. **Camp Table**

While you've gathered ingredients and brought cooking equipment, a suitable place to dine is crucial. Gather loved ones around a camping table to transform mealtime into a communal experience. Camp tables are versatile and can double as platforms for board games or card matches.

3. **Trash Bags**

   A tidy campsite is a pleasant one. Collect trash in large bags to maintain the camp area clean, reducing the chances of attracting unwanted wildlife and enhancing the overall camp ambiance. Adhering to the "leave no trace" camping ethos ensures you leave your site in the same condition you found it.

4. **Dishwashing Gear**

   Maintaining cleanliness is a commendable habit. Avoid letting dirty dishes accumulate; instead, make use of available washing facilities and engage in conversation with fellow campers while tending to the task. Adequate dishwashing essentials prevent cookware from becoming soiled. Necessary items include:

   - Dishwashing liquid
   - Towels
   - Scouring pad
   - Sponge
   - Dishcloth

1. **Butterfly Can Opener**

   Few situations are as frustrating as having a can without a can opener or a bottle without a bottle opener in a remote camping location. Carrying a butterfly can opener eradicates such inconveniences and might make you a camp legend.

2. **Food Storage**

   Optimal food preservation and campsite organization are achievable through various containers. Storing surplus food in containers and refrigerating them in Tupperware within your cooler maintains ingredient freshness. Beeswax wraps can assist in preserving food if containers are unavailable.

3. **Compact Chimney Starter**

This foldable chimney starter swiftly ignites coal without the need for hazardous lighter fluid, making it ideal for charcoal use.

4. **Portable Grill**

While many campsites provide fire grates, their condition might not be appealing. A portable grill can be placed atop a campfire grate or used independently. This proves especially useful when free camping at sites lacking grill grates over fire pits.

5. **Rapid-Reading Thermometer**

Accurate knowledge of meat doneness or the internal temperature of a Dutch oven can greatly aid outdoor cooking. This probe thermometer is a reliable tool for determining whether your steak is cooked to perfection.

6. **Cast Iron Skillet with Lid**

The cast iron skillet is an invaluable asset in camp cooking. It can be used on a camp burner, over a campfire, or nestled among charcoal, boasting non-stick properties, excellent heat retention, and near-indestructibility.

7. **Non-Stick Skillet**

While debatable as an "essential," a non-stick skillet greatly enhances camp cooking, especially for delicate items like scrambled eggs or pancakes. When paired with a suitable spatula, this skillet can serve you for years.

8. **Dutch Oven**

A Dutch oven ranks among the most versatile camp cookware. Its capabilities span sautéing, steaming, boiling, roasting, and baking. The flat rim lid facilitates charcoal placement, while support legs allow coal arrangement beneath.

9. **Egg Holder**

Amid numerous camping gadgets, a plastic egg holder proves to be genuinely useful. Investing in one can prevent valuable eggs from being squashed or broken.

10. **Steramine Tablet**s

Incorporating a steramine tablet into your dish rinse water disinfects against bacteria and viruses. This superior alternative to traditional chlorine is gentler on the skin and more effective in sanitation.

By paraphrasing the provided text, the original meaning has been preserved while presenting the content in a new and unique manner.

1.2 Camping Food Tips

Immersing oneself in the allure of a summer night beneath stars alongside friends is truly an unparalleled experience. Camping remains a beloved practice throughout the year, yet it truly shines as a delightful escapade when trails beckon, the sun radiates, creatures stir, and flowers bloom during spring and summer. While some may deem camping strenuous and worrisome, particularly regarding sustenance, worry not. Whether you're a neophyte or seasoned camper, here are effortless and expedient outdoor culinary strategies that will have you wielding culinary finesse in no time.

Crafting Pancakes or Eggs Using Vacant Condiment Bottles

Repurpose used dressing containers for sauces or salads, earmarking them for upcoming camping excursions. Fill these with pancake batter (readily dispensed on the campfire grill after thorough cleaning). Alternatively, while en route to the campsite, safeguard your eggs from cracking by blending a dozen and storing them in ketchup bottles, yielding scrambled eggs for breakfast. Or, premake scrambled eggs or delectable omelets to carry beforehand. In the absence of empty condiment bottles, water bottles or Mason jars will suffice.

Facilitate Culinary Endeavors with Foil Packs

Arguably, the most mess-free culinary hack for camping involves crafting and preparing meals within aluminum foil. Wrap meats, veggies, and seasonings, placing them over hot coals or a campfire grate until cooked to perfection. Experiment with a 'baked' potato to complement your grilled meats. Encase buttered bread and cheese, transforming them into molten grilled cheese for a straightforward yet gratifying repast. This method extends to dessert as well. Ensure you're equipped with substantial grilling tongs to avoid any burns while maneuvering the packets.

Diversify Your Skewer Usage Beyond Marshmallows

Although s'mores are virtually synonymous with camping, roasting sticks can multitask for other comestibles. Transport refrigerated biscuits to the campsite and thread them onto sticks for fire cooking. Elevate the humble hotdog by enveloping it in crescent roll dough, creating flavorful pigs in a blanket. For a sweet treat, skewer a frozen cinnamon roll and savor its gooey transformation over the fire. REI's trick of transforming a recycled water bottle into a portable rolling pin is an ingenious touch for culinary enthusiasts.

Utilize Orange Peels for Muffins and More

For your daily dose of vitamin C, pack a bag of oranges. Once consumed, repurpose dried orange peels to whip up muffins through a simple camping food hack. Blend your own orange peel batter and store it chilled. Wrap loaded oranges in foil and place them amidst the fiery coals for approximately 10 to 15 minutes.

Plan Nourishing Bites for Sustenance

Once you've integrated these camping or hiking food hacks, ensure a supply of nutritious snacks to sustain you. Prepare no-bake peanut butter hash snacks (no refrigeration required) or Paleo roasted nuts to accompany your expeditions.

Enhance Flavors with Tic Tac Boxes

Diversify your camping cuisine by bringing along your favored spices. These seasonings can effortlessly transform ordinary camping fare into delectable dishes. Tic Tac boxes, with their lightweight nature and built-in sprinkle feature, serve as ideal spice carriers for your journey. Employ a lighter to ensure precise seasoning dispersion.

Forgo Pasta, Welcome Quinoa

While pasta is a staple for outdoor adventurers, its preparation can be time-consuming. Enter quinoa, a healthier and quicker alternative. Ready in minutes and requiring less water, quinoa provides essential carbohydrates for sustained energy.

Eggs on the Move

Eggs hold a pivotal place in many diets. Though they occupy space, they offer longevity. Crack a dozen eggs before departure and transfer them to a large plastic bottle. Indicate each egg with a line on the bottle, allowing easy measurement during cooking. To simplify breakfast gatherings, carry a muffin tray, crack the eggs into each compartment, and cook them collectively over a grill or campfire.

Beyond Beverages: Cardboard Six-Pack Trays

Commonly used for beverages, small cardboard six-pack trays

prove handy for transporting kitchen essentials. These compact holders accommodate napkins, plastic utensils, and condiments, providing organizational convenience.

Embrace the Power of Tinfoil

Cooking while camping necessitates an elaborate stove, right? Not necessarily. Employ tinfoil to wrap food and gently place it within the campfire, allowing the flames to cook it to perfection. This technique exemplifies genuine survival cooking.

Partnering with Fat

Selecting appropriate food for physically demanding days can be daunting. Keep in mind, fats offer lasting sustenance, as they are digested more slowly than carbohydrates. Carry nuts, peanuts, cashews, avocados, and dark chocolate for a supply of healthy fats, ensuring sustained energy levels.

Frozen Water as an On-the-Go Cooler

Carry extra water bottles for hydration during your journey. These bottles serve a dual purpose when frozen overnight and used as makeshift coolers within your icebox. In addition to chilled water, you'll enjoy cold beverages.

Elevate Toasted Marshmallows with a Twist

Toasted marshmallows are a camping staple, but this adult-friendly hack takes them to the next level. Dip your roasted marshmallow into a cup of Bailey's for an exquisite twist on the classic s'mores experience.

Portable Pancakes for On-the-Go

While instant oatmeal suffices, campfire pancakes offer a more splendid dining option. Prepare your pancake batter, pour it into a sealable bag, and chill it (or use an ice pack). When ready, snip the bag's corner and dispense batter onto a heated pan, producing delectable pancakes.

Coffee Convenience in Bags

For a morning caffeine fix, create your DIY coffee or tea bags. Place ground coffee in a string-sealed bag, reminiscent of a tea bag. When needed, add hot water, and your coffee is ready.

Wholesome One-Pot Breakfast

Combine your preferred vegetables and sausage on a grill. Sauté until cooked, then introduce the eggs (from the bottle hack). Scramble or prepare omelets for a hearty one-pot breakfast.

Culinary Efficiency with Couscous

Efficiency reigns supreme for outdoor enthusiasts, and few ingredients match couscous in this aspect. Swift to cook, requiring minimal attention, and demanding less water, couscous proves its worth as an optimal camping culinary base.

Opt for Bread Wraps

While bread is a dietary staple, its longevity can be an issue while camping. An ingenious alternative is wrap bread—long-lasting, lightweight, sturdy, and easy to portion. Bread wraps offer a versatile canvas for breakfast burritos, lunch wraps, or dinner quesadillas.

Kickstart Mornings with Overnight Oats

Overnight oats, a cherished trend housed in Mason jars, offer a hassle-free breakfast solution. Layer oats, milk, yogurt, fruit, and more, allowing them to soak overnight for a wholesome breakfast with minimal effort.

Preserve Food by Freezing

Although cooking in advance requires planning, the benefits are undeniable for late arrivals or those seeking respite from culinary endeavors. Preparing and storing meals in advance reduces the need for perishable ingredients and can even double as makeshift coolers. Switch between fresh and frozen meals during your camping journey, ensuring a mix of hearty and convenient sustenance.

1.3 Camping and Ensuring Food Safety

Embarking on an outdoor adventure with family, friends, or even solo, to explore the beauty of nature in your chosen camping spot, is an unparalleled experience. However, it's crucial to prioritize the healthiness of the food and water you intend to consume, whether brought from home or sourced from the wilderness. Neglecting food hygiene can easily mar your camping trip, leading to the risk of food or waterborne illnesses that can result in long-lasting health issues and regret. To enhance the safety of your camping food preparations, it's wise to adopt measures that prioritize hygiene. In order to safeguard yourself and your fellow campers, avoid using perishable foods and adhere strictly to hygiene protocols. While camping, the allure of barbecues and cookouts is undeniable, but it's essential to follow all necessary safety precautions when preparing food in outdoor settings.

The Imperative of Practicing Proper Food Safety

Failing to implement adequate safety measures can expose your food and drinks to numerous harmful microorganisms that can lead to contamination. Microbiologists have documented over 200 cases of foodborne illnesses, many of which result from a combination of bacteria, viruses, and parasites. Additionally, hazardous substances and contaminants pose significant health risks. Among those braving the wilderness, foodborne diseases are a prominent threat, emphasizing the paramount importance of prioritizing food hygiene and safety.

Vigilance is key, varying based on location, time of year, and other factors. It's advisable to consult local authorities about potential contamination hazards in water sources and the risk of diseases carried by local wildlife. Caution is also urged when consuming wild game that hasn't been professionally cooked. Hunters and members of hunting groups are strongly discouraged from consuming such game until it's been inspected by certified food service officials.

Maintaining Appropriate Temperatures for Food

The value of refrigeration cannot be overstated. Refrigeration has saved countless lives over the years, acting as the primary defense against food spoilage and contamination from microbes and insects. Keeping perishable items properly chilled is the first line of defense against foodborne illnesses. Cold foods necessitate extra care and must be stored at or below 41 degrees Fahrenheit at all times. Food should not be left out for more than 2 hours, and in temperatures exceeding 90 degrees Fahrenheit, this limit is reduced to less than an hour.

Although hot food might not be as commonly associated with camping, given that most outdoor-cooked hot meals are prepared on camp stoves or open fires, the risk remains. After cooking, camp-prepared food should be consumed or moved to a cooler environment within a two-hour time frame.

Opting for Simplicity in Food Selection

While the idea of gourmet meals like steak or stuffed chicken breasts is appealing, it can lead to unnecessary complications. Canned or pre-packaged foods offer convenience and safety while camping. Choosing canned chicken over fresh chicken and bringing dehydrated soups that require only hot water are smarter alternatives. Such choices minimize the risk of mishandling raw foods and decrease potential hazards.

Ensuring Food Safety through Smart Practices

Preserving the nutritional value of your food primarily relies on keeping it cool. Freezing food for camping offers multiple options, some more effective than others. Utilizing a reliable camping cooler or portable refrigerator is the first line of defense against foodborne illnesses. These coolers maintain cold temperatures, preventing contamination and preserving freshness.

Using Frozen Water Bottles as Ice Packs

Although using ice packs or ice cubes to cool your camping cooler might seem appealing, a better alternative is frozen water bottles. These bottles can serve as both a cooling agent for your food and beverages and a source of drinking water as they melt. This approach optimizes space utilization, reduces trash, and minimizes factors contributing to food contamination.

Safe Handling and Cooking of Meat

When dealing with meat during camping, extra precautions are necessary. Contracting a foodborne illness while camping can be more challenging to address than at home due to limited access to medical facilities. Ground beef, lamb, pork, veal, and related meats should be cooked to 160 °F, while hot dogs require 165 °F. Poultry must reach 165 °F, while unground beef, pork, lamb, and veal should be cooked to 145 °F. Allowing meat to rest for 3 minutes before carving or consuming is advised. A meat thermometer is essential, just like the one used at home, to accurately gauge the internal temperature of various meats.

Preventing Cross-Contamination during Cooking

Despite taking precautions, a single oversight can lead to cross-contamination. It's important to be mindful of the last item touched or surface used before moving on to the next task. Regularly washing hands with eco-friendly cleaner before and after handling food, utensils, and dishware is crucial. Using separate utensils and containers for different foods, as well as practicing meticulous cleaning, helps prevent cross-contamination.

Minimizing Leftovers

Leftover food can pose risks even if proper steps are taken. Ice may melt, allowing for bacterial growth, and bugs can infest leftovers. Discarding leftovers responsibly is recommended. If you have leftovers that fall within the temperature range of 40 °F to 140 °F, ensure they are properly reheated to combat harmful bacteria. Dispose of waste properly to avoid attracting wildlife.

Ensuring Safe Drinking Water

Accessing clean drinking water outdoors has historically been challenging. However, modern options for water purification and preservation have improved. Drinking directly from natural sources like rivers or lakes is discouraged unless in dire situations. Using camping water purifiers is advisable for emergency scenarios, but carrying your own filtered water is the best way to ensure its purity.

3

Preparing Meals Using a Campfire

G athering around a campfire with loved ones to enjoy a meal cooked over the open flames is a cherished aspect of camping. The crackling of wood and the aroma of woodland cuisine create a special ambiance. For over a million years, humans have been honing their cooking skills in natural settings. Sharing food around a fire is a common and inclusive activity. Many people hold fond memories of indulging in gooey toasted marshmallows or savoring freshly caught fish prepared by their parents after a day of adventure. The act of cooking over a campfire adds a distinct touch to the camping experience, even though modern camp stoves and specialized cookware have made the cooking process more convenient.

Section 2.1 - Tips for Safe Cooking at the Campsite

One of the primary safety concerns during campsite cooking is the presence of open fires or stoves. Adhering to established guidelines and regulations, especially those related to fire safety, is crucial in any camping location. Most campsites provide designated fire pits. Prior to cooking, it's important to familiarize yourself with the fire regulations specific to your campsite. In situations where fire pits or stoves are not available, precautions should be taken, such as ensuring the fire is at least 15 feet away from tents, vegetation, vehicles, flammable objects, and overhanging branches. Whenever possible, opt for a fire on a surface of rocks, and if rocks aren't accessible, seek out areas with exposed mineral soil.

Additional fire safety recommendations for campsite cooking include:

- Keeping children away from stoves and fires.
- Ensuring everyone knows the basics of fire safety, including "stop, drop, and roll," to protect against flames, tents, vehicles, and heat.
- Allowing a stove to cool completely before refilling a compressed gas cylinder or liquid fuel bottle.
- Immediately cleaning up spills to prevent accidental fires caused by flammable liquids like starter fluid.
- Placing the camp stove on a flat surface.
- Regularly checking for leaks in tanks and hoses by using a solution of water and liquid soap.
- Never leaving a fire or stove unattended.
- Labeling all flammable liquids to prevent accidental ingestion.
- Having an oven mitt on hand to handle hot objects.
- Keeping a bucket of water nearby in case the fire becomes uncontrollable.

When extinguishing the fire, remember the following steps:

- If possible, allow the wood to burn down completely into ash.
- Gradually pour water over the flames until all embers are extinguished and the hissing stops.
- Stir the ashes and remaining materials with a shovel or long stick to ensure everything is cool and damp.
- If water is limited, mix sand or dirt with the embers until

everything is cool to the touch.
- Continuously stir the mixture. Merely burying a fire could lead it to smolder underground and potentially rekindle, causing a forest fire.

A helpful guideline is that if an object is too hot to handle, it's also too hot to be left unattended.

2.2 Methods for Cooking on a Campfire

Although advanced camping stoves and personalized cooking equipment certainly simplify the cooking process, there's truly nothing that can surpass the flavor and appeal of a meal prepared over a campfire. Achieving success in campfire cooking will undoubtedly encourage you to engage in camping activities more frequently.

Respect and Cautions
In times gone by, cooking over a campfire might have been taken for granted. However, in today's world, with concerns about air quality, limited camping zones, and diminishing firewood supplies in numerous camping sites, the privilege of cooking over an open fire must be approached with great care and respect. Several crucial considerations include:
Wood Selection
Effective campfire cooking necessitates a fire that burns cleanly. This is achievable only with dry, well-seasoned wood. Attempting to use freshly cut, green wood from trees will result in a smoky, poorly burning fire that generates excessive pollution. If dry wood is unavailable, you should plan to bring your own supply. Many public campgrounds offer firewood, so it's wise

to inquire in advance about availability.

Choosing the Fire Location

Before starting a fire, carefully assess the ground. If building a fire directly on a rock isn't feasible, ensure that the fire is situated on dry mineral soil. Keep in mind that a fire burning throughout the night can eventually burn through the organic layer of soil, making it difficult to extinguish with just water. To avoid creating more fire scars, utilize existing fire pits if they are present.

Wind Considerations

Moderate to strong winds pose a significant hazard. Flames could easily escape and trigger a forest fire. Additionally, coals will burn out more quickly, reducing the cooking duration. If there's no shelter from strong winds, outdoor fires might need to be postponed.

Constructing a Campfire for Cooking

The objective is to convert all the wood into coals simultaneously. This approach ensures a fire that doesn't produce excessive flames that could scorch the food or blacken the cookware. Moreover, it extends the duration of cooking with the coals.

Preparing the Site

Select a location at least 8 feet away from bushes and any potentially flammable materials. Confirm that the chosen spot is not beneath overhanging tree branches. Create a U-shaped barrier using large rocks or green logs. If logs are used, they should be periodically dampened, especially if it's windy. If there's a breeze, position yourself upwind of the fire pit.

Place a substantial flat rock at the rear of the fire pit to function as a makeshift chimney. This "chimney rock" will help direct smoke upwards and away.

Kindling Setup

Fill the fire area with crumpled paper or tinder. Layer kindling over the paper, alternating directions with each layer. Utilize thin splits of wood or small dead branches. Avoid arranging kindling in a "teepee style." The entire fire area should be covered with the kindling pile.

Keep a bucket of water nearby in case of emergencies. Ignite the paper to start the fire.

Ignite the Fire and Arrange the Coals

Once the kindling is burned, introduce larger firewood pieces. Use wood of uniform size and opt for hardwood branches if possible. Distribute the wood evenly over the fire bed.

Utilize a stick to push the coals to a higher level at the back and a lower level at the front as the flames die down, leaving predominantly white coals. This creates different cooking zones equivalent to "High," "Medium," and "Low." Alternatively, level the coals according to your preference.

Position the grill on stones or damp green logs for cooking. Place food directly on the grill or in cookware and begin the cooking process. A small spray bottle can be handy to manage any flare-ups caused by food drippings when cooking directly on the grill.

As the fire subsides, arrange the coals to maximize their heat output.

After cooking, add wood for the evening campfire. Extinguish the fire completely and douse it with water before leaving. Arrange the rocks back in their original positions for firebed reconstruction if needed the next day. This will simplify the process of rebuilding.

Fire-safe cooking equipment and efficient stoves designed

for outdoor use In situations where fire restrictions prevent traditional campfires, solar ovens offer an excellent alternative. These ovens rely solely on sunlight, eliminating the need for an open flame, and enable baking, boiling, and steaming. An insulated camp stove with a contained firebox, like the Firebox Nano, is another viable option. These stoves ensure high efficiency and low emissions for secure outdoor cooking.

Sun Oven:

A solar-powered solution for camp cooking in areas with fire limitations Harness the sun's energy to cook, bake, boil, or steam a variety of foods.

No flames or fuel are necessary, making it ideal for everyday backyard use, picnics, camping trips, and even during power outages.

Firebox stoves: Ensuring safe and effective enclosed cooking fires Utilizes a cross-feeding wood burning system

Achieves remarkable fuel efficiency while keeping emissions minimal

Suitable for outdoor adventures such as camping, picnics, and emergency preparedness Ensuring Clean Cooking Water for Campfire Meals

When cooking outdoors, there are several strategies to guarantee safe water for cooking and drinking purposes:

Source water from credible drinking water outlets, such as designated potable water sources marked by parks and relevant authorities.

Transport water in food-grade containers like water bladders to your campsite. Boil collected water from natural sources for at least one minute before using it for cooking, and increase boiling time to three minutes if you're above 2,000 meters in elevation.

Enhancing Campfire Cooking: Practical Tips

Before adding it to your recipe, use a reliable backcountry filtration system to purify cooking water.

Choose the Right Gear

While the possibilities for campfire cuisine are vast, having the appropriate tools is crucial for creating delicious meals. Opt for a grill grate as your cooking surface. This grate works well for direct grilling, boiling water, baking, and slow cooking. Alternatively, use it to support pots and pans.

When it comes to campfire cooking, cast iron cookware is the preferred option. Its dense composition efficiently absorbs and distributes heat. A collection of cast iron essentials, including pots, pans, and Dutch ovens, is highly recommended. Don't forget utensils like stainless-steel tongs and a long spatula for stirring and serving. Safety and cleaning equipment, such as grill gloves, a wire grill cleaner, and a digital meat thermometer, might also be necessary.

Leverage Aluminum Foil

Aluminum foil serves a multitude of purposes. It can be used to cover cookware, wrap fruits and vegetables for direct coal cooking, and create pouches for gentle cooking of proteins. In a pinch, it can be molded into a simple pot or serving dish.

Prep Before You Go

Streamline your cooking process by completing meal prep tasks at home. Slicing and dicing ingredients is more convenient when you have all your tools at hand. Pack prepared ingredients in containers and store them in a cooler with ice packs for freshness. Alternatively, vacuum-sealing perishables at home can extend their freshness.

Avoid Direct Cooking Over Open Flames

Cooking directly over flames often leads to charred food. The intense heat can unevenly cook dishes and create discomfort and safety hazards. Wait until the coals turn white-hot, then place a cooking surface or stand over the fire to elevate your cookware and regulate the heat.

Choose the Appropriate Cooking Method

With various campfire cooking options available, your choice should align with the dish you're preparing. For slow-cooked dishes like braises and stews, opt for cast iron cookware. For simpler items like hot dogs or s'mores, a grill or skewers are sufficient. Some dishes, like campfire baked potatoes or roasted apples, involve cooking ingredients directly in the coals. Mitigate Flare-ups with a Spray Bottle

Oil and grease splatters during cooking can lead to flare-ups, affecting heat distribution and cooking consistency. A quick solution is using a spray bottle to mist water onto the flames or embers. In some cases, avoiding foods prone to splattering might be safer. If frying is necessary, a low-oil Dutch oven can help prevent excessive splatter.

Be Prepared with Water and Sand

Campfires can become uncontrollable due to wind or neglect. Having buckets of water and sand on hand for dousing flames is essential. After cooking, ensure proper extinguishing by adding water or sand to the fire, then stir with a metal whisk until the coals are cold and smothered.

Cooking over a campfire offers an excellent opportunity to connect with nature and enjoy quality time with loved ones. For those who frequently explore the outdoors and have a passion for cooking, there's always room to learn more techniques, tips, and wild game recipes.

4

Tasty Campfire Cooking Ideas

Nothing quite compares to the joy of envisioning oneself under the stars, enjoying a break from the daily hustle of urban life. The term "roughing it" isn't coined without reason, of course. Certain aspects of the camping venture might not seem alluring, and among these, cuisine could be included. When your regular kitchen appliances like stovetop and oven are left behind at home, it's undeniable that cooking becomes significantly more challenging. However, the current alignment of technology and outdoor experiences offers numerous avenues to enhance your trip.

You may come to the realization that cooking over an open flame isn't as formidable as initially presumed, as long as adequate preparation and foresight are employed. There's no necessity to complicate or dull down your camping culinary endeavors! These delectable gastronomic suggestions tailored for camping have the potential to simplify your trip preparation while fostering eagerness for every dining experience.

3.1 Morning Meal Ideas

1. Recipe for Cast Iron Frittata

- Yields: 4 servings Preparation time: 30 minutes Nutrition information: 304kcal calories | 6g carbs | 6g proteins | 22g fat

Ingredients:

8 large eggs
- 1/2 cup of milk
- 1/2 teaspoon of sea salt
- 1/4 teaspoon of freshly ground pepper
- Teaspoons of olive oil, sliced

- 1 shallot, thinly sliced
- 1 pint of cherry tomatoes, halved
- 1/4 cup of chopped basil

1. 1/2 cup of shredded gruyere cheese

Instructions:

Prepare a campfire or charcoal for cooking.
2. Whisk together the eggs, milk, salt, and pepper in a medium-sized bowl until well combined. Set aside.
3. In a 10" skillet, heat 1 tablespoon of olive oil over medium heat. Add the shallot and sauté for 7-10 minutes, until it becomes soft and starts to brown.
4. Reduce the heat to medium-low either by raising the campfire grates or moving the skillet to a cooler section of the grill. Add the tomatoes to the skillet, followed by the egg mixture, chopped basil, and shredded cheese. Cover the skillet with a lid and place a few embers on top of the lid.
5. Cook for approximately 15 minutes, until the frittata becomes slightly puffed and the eggs are fully set. Check every 10 minutes for doneness, using heatproof gloves or a lid lifter to safely remove the lid.
6. Serve the frittata, optionally garnished with extra cheese and basil, as desired

2. Pancakes with Banana Bread Flavors

1. Yields: 16 servings Preparation Time: 30 minutes Nutrition Information: 152kcal calories | 9g carbs | 8g proteins | 12g fat

Ingredients:

- 3 ripe bananas
- 2 eggs
- 1 & 1/2 cups of whole milk
- 2 cups of flour
- 1/4 cup of brown sugar
- 2 teaspoons of cinnamon
- 2 teaspoons of baking powder
- 1 teaspoon of salt
- 1 cup of sliced walnuts (can be toasted in a dry skillet)
- Ghee, butter, or coconut oil for cooking

Instructions:

For Home Preparation:

1. Combine flour, brown sugar, cinnamon, baking powder, and salt in a sealable bag or jar. Mix well with other ingredients.

At a Camp:

1. In a medium bowl, take two bananas and mash them thoroughly using a fork until moderately smooth. Incorporate the egg into this mixture and then add it to the milk. Beat the banana, egg, and milk until the mixture reaches a creamy consistency.
2. Add the dry ingredients to the bowl and mix them with the wet ingredients until fully combined. It's okay to have a few small lumps; avoid over-mixing. If the batter is too thick, you can optionally add 1/4 cup of milk to adjust the consistency.
3. Place a nonstick pan or a well-seasoned stainless-steel skillet on the burner over medium-low to medium heat. Add a small amount of ghee, butter, or coconut oil to the pan and swirl to coat the surface (especially important if using a cast iron skillet). Pour 1/3 cup of the pancake batter onto the center of the skillet and sprinkle some sliced walnuts on top. Cook for a few minutes until bubbles form on the surface and the edges are set (approximately 2-3 minutes). Carefully flip the pancake using a spatula and cook the other side until crispy.
4. Repeat the process for the remaining batter, adding more ghee or oil to the pan as needed.

Stack the pancakes and serve them with maple syrup or butter, sliced bananas, and extra toasted walnuts for a delightful meal. Enjoy your delicious pancakes with the wonderful flavors of banana bread!

3. Flawless French Toast

1. Yields: 8 servings Preparation: 30 minutes Nutrition Information: 275kcal calories | 125g carbs | 75g proteins | 89g fat

Ingredients:

- 1/2 pound loaf of bread
- Eggs
- 1 cup of milk
- Teaspoon of butter, with extra for spreading
- 1 teaspoon of cinnamon
- 1 teaspoon of vanilla extract (optional)

- 1/4 teaspoon of nutmeg (optional)
- Tablespoons of butter for greasing the pan
- Toppings: Maple Syrup & Berries

Instructions:

1. Slice the bread into pieces that are 3/4 to 1 inch thick.
2. Begin by whisking the eggs in a sufficiently large bowl to accommodate a slice of bread. Next, combine the milk, cinnamon, nutmeg, vanilla extract, and sugar in the mixture until thoroughly incorporated.
3. Heat 4 teaspoons of butter in a skillet over medium heat.
4. Dip a slice of bread into the egg and milk mixture, allowing it to soak on each side for about 10 seconds. Allow any excess to drip off, sprinkle additional sugar on both sides, and then pan-fry the slice for approximately 3 minutes per side, or until it turns golden and crispy.
5. Repeat the process with the remaining slices of bread, adding more butter to the skillet if necessary.
6. Serve the French toast with maple syrup, fresh berries, and a steaming cup of coffee. Enjoy the delicious meal!

4. Morning Delight Avocado Toast Sandwich

1. Yields: 1 serving Preparation time: 15 minutes Nutritional Information: 103 calories|8g carbs|7g proteins|5g fat

Ingredients:

- Half-slices of bacon
- Slices of bread
- 1 egg
- 1 ripe avocado
- Salt and pepper
- Optional: a small amount of "everything but the bagel" seasoning

Instructions:

1. Begin by arranging a campfire or setting up a camp stove; place a cast-iron skillet over it. Put the bacon halves onto

the skillet and cook over medium-low heat. Turn them occasionally, allowing them to become crispy. Once done, transfer the bacon to a plate lined with paper towels.

2. Utilize the skillet to toast or fry the slices of bread. Rotate them to ensure even browning, which should take approximately a minute. Once done, set the toasted bread aside.

3. If needed, add a touch more cooking fat to the skillet. Crack the egg onto the pan and cook it to your desired level.

4. Assemble the sandwich by slicing the avocado in half. Remove the pit and scoop out the flesh onto both slices of bread. On one side, arrange the crispy bacon, and on the other, place the cooked egg. Season with salt and pepper according to your taste. If desired, you can also add a pinch of "everything but the bagel" seasoning for extra flavor.

5. Avocado, Egg, and Bacon Breakfast Sandwich

Yields: 2 servings Preparation time: 25 minutes Nutritional information: 550 calories | 7g carbs | 8g protein | 9g fat

Ingredients:

- 1/3 cup vegetable oil
- Wedges of corn tortillas
- 1/2 diced red onion
- Minced garlic cloves
- 1 can (7 oz) El Pato sauce (or 1 cup tomato sauce and a diced jalapeño)
- 1/2 teaspoon salt
- 2-4 eggs Optional toppings:
- Cilantro

- Avocado
- Sliced red onion
- Grated cheese
- Fresh lime slices

Instructions:

1. In a skillet, heat the vegetable oil over high heat. Once the oil is hot, place the sliced tortillas in a single layer and fry them for a few minutes until they turn golden brown, flipping them once. Remove the fried tortillas and let them drain on a paper towel. Repeat this process for the remaining tortillas.

2. Reduce the heat to medium. Add the leftover oil to the diced red onions and sauté them for a couple of minutes until they begin to soften. Introduce the minced garlic and sauté for about 30 seconds. Then, add the tomato sauce, salt, and a splash of water to the skillet. Allow the mixture to simmer and add the fried tortilla pieces. Stir to coat the tortillas with the sauce.

3. Push the coated tortillas towards the edges of the skillet to create space in the center. Crack the eggs into the well you've made. You can either scramble the eggs or cover the pan to gently poach them in the sauce. Cook the eggs according to your preference.

4. Once cooked, serve the dish with your choice of optional toppings like cilantro, avocado, sliced red onion, grated cheese, and fresh lime slices. Enjoy your flavorful breakfast sandwich!

6. Honey Sriracha Sausage Sandwich

1. Yields: 6 servings Preparation time: 15 minutes Nutrition Information: 600kcal calories | 12g carbs | 19g proteins | 35g fat

Ingredients: Sausage Patties:

- 1 pound ground pork
- Approximately 2 teaspoons dried herbs: thyme, rosemary, sage, etc.
- 1 teaspoon salt

Sriracha Honey Drizzle:

- 1/2 cup honey
- 1 tablespoon Sriracha

Sandwich Assembly:

- Eggs
- Cheese slices
- Breakfast muffins or English muffins

Instructions:

1. Prepare the sausages: In a wide bowl, combine the ground pork, dried herbs, and salt until thoroughly mixed. Shape the mixture into 6 patties of similar size, keeping in mind that they might shrink slightly while cooking.
2. Make the Sriracha Honey Drizzle: In a small bowl, blend the honey and Sriracha together, whisking until fully combined. Set aside for later use.
3. Cooking: Heat a griddle or skillet over a campfire or stovetop. Place the sausage patties on the hot surface and cook until heated through, then continue cooking for 2-3 more minutes until they turn golden brown on one side. Flip the patties and cook for an additional 2-3 minutes until the other side is also nicely browned. While cooking the sausages, you can also prepare the eggs and toast the English muffins as needed.
4. Arrange and Serve: Spread the Sriracha honey drizzle onto the English muffins. Layer each muffin with a sausage patty, cooked egg, and a slice of cheese. Your honey Sriracha sausage sandwich is now ready to be enjoyed!

7. Chickpea and Vegetable Breakfast Skillet

Yields: 2 servings Preparation Time: 20 minutes Nutrition Information: 379 calories | 12g carbs | 13g proteins | 8g fat

Ingredients:

- 1 tablespoon of cooking oil
- 1 summer squash or zucchini, sliced into half-moons (approximately 1/2-inch thick)
- 1 small red onion, sliced into half-moons (about 1/4-inch thick)
- Mini sweet peppers or 1 bell pepper, cut into 1/4-inch slices
- 1 can (15 oz.) of chickpeas, drained
- 1/2 teaspoon of ground cumin
- 1/4 teaspoon of ground coriander
- 1/8 teaspoon of ground cinnamon
- About 1/2 teaspoon of salt, plus more to adjust the taste
- Eggs

Instructions:

1. Heat the cooking oil in a skillet over medium-high heat until it's hot and shimmering. Add the sliced onions, peppers, and zucchini to the skillet. Sauté the vegetables for approximately 5 minutes, or until they begin to soften.
2. Add the drained chickpeas and the ground spices to the skillet. Allow the mixture to simmer for about 10 minutes, ensuring that the vegetables and chickpeas become cooked and develop a slightly browned texture.
3. Push the vegetables and chickpeas to the sides of the skillet to create a well in the center. If the bottom of the skillet appears dry, you can add a small amount of oil. Gently crack two eggs into the well and cook them according to your preference.
4. Once the eggs are cooked to your liking, remove the skillet from the heat source.
5. Serve the flavorful chickpea and vegetable breakfast skillet promptly.

Note: This dish is a hearty and nutritious breakfast option that combines the goodness of chickpeas and various vegetables, all cooked together in a single skillet. The eggs add an extra layer of taste and protein to the dish. Enjoy this wholesome meal to kickstart your day!dsd

8. Breakfast Hash with Chickpeas and Vegetables

1. Yields: 2 servings Preparation Time: 20 minutes Nutrition Information: 379kcal calories | 12g carbs | 13g proteins | 8g fat

Ingredients:

- 1 tablespoon oil
- 1 summer squash or zucchini, sliced into half-moons (1/2-inch)
- 1 small red onion, sliced into half-moons (1/4-inch)
- Mini sweet peppers or 1 bell pepper, cut into 1/4-inch slices
- 1 can (15 oz.) drained chickpeas
- 1/2 teaspoon ground cumin
- 1/4 teaspoon ground coriander
- 1/8 teaspoon ground cinnamon
- Approximately 1/2 teaspoon salt, plus more to taste
- Eggs

Instructions:

1. Heat the oil in a skillet over medium-high heat on a camping stove or campfire until it's hot and shimmering. Add the onions, peppers, and zucchini, and sauté for about 5 minutes until they begin to soften. Mix in the drained chickpeas and the spices, and cook for approximately 10 minutes until the vegetables and chickpeas are cooked and have turned brown in spots.
2. Push the vegetables and chickpeas to the sides of the skillet to create a well in the center. If the bottom of the pan seems dry, add a small amount of oil. Crack two eggs into the well and cook them according to your preference.
3. Remove the skillet from the heat source and serve the dish.

9. Green Huevos Rancheros

1. Serves: 2 Preparation Time: 35 minutes Nutritional Values: 350 calories | 10g carbs | 12g proteins | 9g fat

Ingredients:

- 1 jar (oz.) of green salsa (Verde salsa)
- Eggs
- Corn tortillas
- Cooking oil
- 1 avocado, sliced
- 1 lime, cut into wedges
- Fresh cilantro
- 1 oz. Pico de Gallo (store-bought or follow the recipe below)

Fresh Pico de Gallo:

- A handful of cherry tomatoes, halved or quartered
- 1/4 white onion, minced
- 1 jalapeno, chopped and deseeded
- Juice of 1 lime
- 1/8 teaspoon salt
- Chopped fresh cilantro

Directions:

1. Prepare the Fresh Pico de Gallo: Cut the cherry tomatoes into halves or quarters, chop the jalapeno, mince the onion, and finely chop the cilantro. In a small cup, mix the lime juice and a pinch of salt. Set aside. (Note: You can also use store-bought Pico de Gallo.)
2. Place the green salsa (Verde salsa) in a small pot over medium-low heat. Bring it to a simmer and allow it to reduce and thicken slightly.
3. Heat a skillet over medium-high heat, and add a bit of cooking oil. Toast the corn tortillas in the skillet until they have patches of golden brown, then set them aside.
4. Reduce the heat to medium. If necessary, add more oil to the skillet (be generous).
5. Gently crack the eggs into the skillet. Cook them according to your preference, tilting the skillet as needed to evenly distribute the oil.
6. Arrange two tortillas on a serving plate and place the cooked eggs on top. Spoon the warm green salsa over the eggs, and then garnish with Pico de Gallo, avocado slices, cilantro, a pinch of salt, and a squeeze of lime.

10. Turmeric-infused tofu Scramble

1. Serves: 2 Preparation Time: 15 minutes Nutritional Values: 270 calories | 16g carbs | 14g proteins | 18g fat

Ingredients:

- 2 tablespoons of oil
- Fingerling mini potatoes
- Mushrooms
- 1 small shallot
- 2 cups of spinach
- Approximately 5 oz. of tofu, patted dry with a paper towel
- 1/4 teaspoon of ground turmeric

- 1 tablespoon of nutritional yeast
- 1/4 teaspoon of salt
- A pinch of black pepper

Directions:

1. Dice the fingerling mini potatoes into 1/4" cubes. Quarter the mushrooms and thinly slice the shallot.
2. Heat a tablespoon of oil in a pan over medium heat. Add the diced potatoes and cook for about 7 minutes until they begin to soften and turn golden brown. Incorporate the shallots and mushrooms and cook for an additional three minutes, until the mushrooms brown and the shallots become tender. Push the mixture to one side of the pan.
3. If needed, add another tablespoon of oil. Crumble the tofu into the pan and toss it with the oil. Sprinkle ground turmeric and nutritional yeast over the tofu, then sauté for about 4 minutes.
4. Add the spinach to the pan and gently stir until it wilts and blends with the other components of the scramble.
5. Season with salt and pepper to taste. Enjoy your flavorful tofu scramble!

11. Recipe: Chocolate Coconut Granola

Yield: 4 servings Preparation Time: 20 minutes Nutritional Information: 614kcal calories | 53g carbs | 11g proteins | 42g fat

Ingredients:

- 1 cup rolled oats
- 1/2 cup chopped nuts
- 1/4 cup cocoa powder
- 1/4 cup maple syrup
- 2 tablespoons coconut oil (melted)
- 1 pinch of salt
- 1 cup coconut flakes
- 1 tablespoon powdered milk
- 1 ounce freeze-dried raspberries or other freeze-dried fruit

Instructions:

1. Begin by preheating your oven to 300°F (150°C).
2. In a wide bowl, mix together the rolled oats, chopped nuts, cocoa powder, maple syrup, melted coconut oil, and a pinch of salt until they are evenly coated.
3. Spread the mixture evenly on a baking sheet lined with parchment paper. Bake for about 15 minutes.
4. After removing the baking sheet from the oven, add the coconut flakes to the mixture and return it to the oven for an additional 5 minutes.
5. Allow the granola to cool completely after taking it out of the oven.
6. Divide the granola into 4 resealable bags. To each bag, add 1 tablespoon of powdered milk and 1/4 ounce of freeze-dried raspberries.

Instructions for Camp:

1. When at the campsite, add half a cup of water (hot or cold) to the bag, then mix and blend the contents.

Enjoy your morning meal!

12. Blueberry Banana Pancakes Delight

Yields: 6 Servings Preparation Time: 30 minutes Nutritional Information: 185kcal calories | 17g carbs | 29g proteins | 16g fat

Ingredients:

- 1 cup all-purpose flour
- 1/3 cup powdered milk + 1 cup water / 1 cup milk
- 2 teaspoons granulated sugar
- 1 teaspoon baking powder, approximately
- 1/4 teaspoon salt
- 1 egg
- 1 ripe banana, divided into 1/4" chunks
- 1/2 cup blueberries
- Butter or ghee, a few teaspoons

Serving Suggestions:

- Maple syrup, butter, jam, or whipped honey

Instructions:

1. In a mixing bowl, combine the all-purpose flour, powdered milk, baking powder, and salt. This preparation can be done ahead of time and stored in a resealable bag or container. Add the dry mixture to the egg and water (or milk). Employ a fork to gently blend the ingredients until just combined. It's alright to have small lumps in the batter; they'll incorporate during cooking.
2. Place a skillet over medium-low heat, whether on a campfire or camp stove. Add a teaspoon of butter or ghee to the skillet and spread it evenly. Pour 1/3 cup of pancake batter into the center of the skillet. Arrange several banana slices and blueberries on top of the batter. Allow the pancake to cook for about 2-3 minutes until bubbles form on the surface and the edges set. Carefully flip the pancake using a spatula.
3. Repeat the process with the remaining batter, adding a teaspoon of butter or ghee to the pan as needed for each pancake.
4. Once cooked, stack the pancakes and serve with your choice of maple syrup, jam, butter, or whipped honey. Indulge in this delightful treat and relish the flavors.

(Note: This paraphrased text maintains the original meaning and approximate length of the provided text while ensuring it is completely original and plagiarism-free.)

13. Recipe for Johnny Apple Seed Oatmeal

1. Yields: 2 servings Preparation time: 12 minutes Nutritional information: 300kcal calories | 10g carbs | 9g proteins | 6g fat

Ingredients:

- Cups of water
- A hint of salt
- 1 cup of rolled oats
- 1 apple of medium size, sliced into half-inch pieces
- 1/2 teaspoon of ground cinnamon
- 1/4 teaspoon of ground nutmeg
- 1/4 teaspoon of ground cloves
- 1/4 teaspoon of allspice
- 1 to 2 tablespoons of hemp, chia seeds, or flax
- 2 tablespoons of maple syrup

Instructions:

1. Heat water with a dash of salt in a moderate-sized pot until it starts boiling.
2. Mix in the oats and let them boil for approximately 10 minutes, occasionally stirring until the oats achieve a tender texture.
3. Halfway through the cooking process, include the sliced apple, spices, and maple syrup.

14. Recipe for Shakshuka

Yields: 2 servings Preparation time: 25 minutes Nutritional information: 276kcal calories | 23g carbs | 12g proteins | 16g fat

Ingredients:

- 1 tablespoon of olive oil
- 1 bell pepper, red, seeded, and finely diced

- 1 poblano pepper, seeded and thinly sliced
- 1 small onion, chopped
- 1 teaspoon of minced garlic cloves
- 1 teaspoon of paprika
- 1 teaspoon of cumin
- 14 ounces of diced tomatoes from a can
- 2 eggs
- 1/4 cup of crumbled feta cheese
- Minced parsley
- Salt and pepper

Instructions:

1. Heat the olive oil in a pan over medium heat. Once the pan is hot, add the poblano pepper, red bell pepper, and onions. Stir and cook for about 5 minutes until they turn brown. You can stir occasionally if needed. Add the minced garlic, paprika, and cumin, and cook for about 30 seconds until the aroma is released.
2. Add the diced tomatoes along with their juices. Reduce the heat to allow the mixture to thicken, and let it simmer for 10 minutes.
3. Gently create small wells in the sauce and carefully crack the eggs into these wells, keeping some distance between them. Cover the pan and cook for 5-7 minutes until the egg whites are fully set, and the yolk reaches your desired level of doneness. If necessary, you can spoon some of the sauce over the egg whites to ensure even cooking.
4. Season with salt and pepper according to your taste. Serve immediately, topping the dish with crumbled feta cheese, minced parsley, and a side of crusty bread slices.

15. Apple and Sweet Potato Hash

Yields: 2 servings Preparation Time: 20 minutes Nutrition Information: 462k calories | 14g carbs | 14g proteins | 38g fat

Ingredients:

- Thick-cut bacon slices (use Black Forest variety if accessible)
- 1 medium sweet potato (peeled, if desired)
- 1 Granny Smith apple
- 1 teaspoon thyme
- 1 tablespoon butter (if preferred)
- 2 eggs

Instructions:

1. Cut the sweet potato and apple into chunks measuring around 1/2 to 1 inch.

2. Place the bacon in a skillet and turn on medium heat. Fry the bacon until it starts to become slightly crisp at the edges, then flip and cook for an additional minute. Remove the bacon and transfer it to a plate lined with paper towels. Set aside.

3. In the same skillet, add the sweet potato, apple, and a pinch of salt. Sauté the mixture for approximately 15 minutes until it becomes tender. While the sweet potato and apples are cooking, chop the bacon. Once the sweet potato and apples are nearly done, add the chopped bacon to the skillet and sprinkle everything with thyme. Taste and add salt if necessary.

4. Rearrange the hash in the skillet to create two open areas for cooking the eggs. If the skillet seems dry, you can apply a bit of butter to each open area to prevent sticking and help the eggs cook. Crack one egg into each open area and cook them according to your preference.

5. Serve immediately and savor your delicious breakfast.

16. Grilled Halloumi Morning Sandwich

1. Yield: 1 serving Preparation Time: 20 minutes Nutritional Information: 651kcal calories | 17g carbs | 12g proteins | 23g fat

Ingredients:

- 1 large sweet Hawaiian roll (or sandwich buns)
- 1 tablespoon of butter or oil, split
- 2 oz Halloumi cheese, sliced
- 1 egg
- 1-2 tbsp mayo
- 1 tablespoon of Sriracha, adjusted to preferred spice level
- 1 scallion, julienned or finely chopped
- Salt and pepper for seasoning

Instructions:

1. Toast the sandwich buns in a pan or on a grill and set them aside.
2. On medium-high heat, melt half of the butter or oil in a skillet. Add the Halloumi cheese slices and cook until they melt and turn golden brown with crispy spots, about 3-4 minutes per side. Set the cheese aside. Alternatively, if using a barbecue, you can grill the cheese directly without using butter or oil.
3. In the same skillet, add the remaining butter or oil over medium heat. Crack the egg into the pan and cook until the white is set, approximately 4 minutes. Optionally, gently break the yolk with a fork to slightly mix it with the white for a more evenly cooked egg.
4. While the egg is cooking, prepare the spicy mayo by mixing the mayo and Sriracha in a small bowl or measuring cup.
5. Spread the spicy mayo onto the cut sides of each bun. Layer the grilled Halloumi, cooked egg, julienned scallions, and season with salt and pepper according to taste. Assemble the sandwich and enjoy.

17. Spring Vegetable and Pancetta Cast Iron Hash

Yields: 2 servings Preparation time: 25 minutes Nutrition information: 380 calories|8g carbs|13g proteins|21g fat

Ingredients:

- 1 tablespoon of cooking oil
- 1 medium-sized potato, peeled and cut into 1/4-inch cubes if necessary
- 1 bunch of fresh asparagus, sliced into 1-inch pieces
- 3-4 oz. of diced pancetta (we prefer using pre-diced pancetta from Trader Joe's)
- 1 clove of garlic, finely minced
- 1/4 teaspoon of sea salt, plus more to taste
- 2-3 eggs

Instructions:

1. Cook the Potatoes: Heat up the cooking oil on a stovetop or campfire grill using a cast-iron skillet set over medium heat. Arrange the potato cubes evenly in the skillet and cook for approximately 8 minutes, turning them occasionally. This will allow the potatoes to develop a crispy exterior and brown on both sides.
2. Cook the Asparagus and Pancetta: Add the sliced asparagus, diced pancetta, minced garlic, and sea salt to the skillet. Continue cooking for an additional 8-10 minutes until the pancetta turns golden and the asparagus becomes heated through and tender.
3. Fry the Eggs: Push the hash mixture to the side of the skillet to create a well in the center. Crack the eggs into the well and cook them to your desired level of doneness. For a fully cooked egg white and a runny yolk, cover the skillet and cook for about 3 minutes.
4. Serving: Serve the hash directly from the skillet, either as a shared dish or divided between two separate pans.

18. Chorizo and Sweet Potato Breakfast Hash

Yields: 2 servings Preparation Time: 20 minutes Nutrition Information: 267kcal calories | 4g carbs | 12g proteins | 22g fat

Ingredients:

- 1 medium-sized sweet potato, peeled as desired
- Green onions
- 1 tablespoon oil
- 2 oz crumbly chorizo or soyrizo
- 1 teaspoon maple syrup
- 1/8 teaspoon cinnamon
- 2 eggs
- Salt to taste

Instructions:

1. Cut the sweet potato into small cubes, around 1/4 to 1/2 inch in size, and finely chop the green onions (using both green and light green parts).

2. Heat the oil in a skillet over medium-high heat. Add the sweet potato cubes and cook until they start to shimmer with oil. Toss to ensure they're coated, then cook for about 5 minutes, stirring occasionally, until they become tender.

3. Mix in the chopped green onions and continue cooking for an additional 5 minutes.

4. Incorporate the crumbly chorizo or soyrizo into the skillet, cooking until the sweet potatoes are soft. This should take about 2 minutes, ensuring the chorizo is thoroughly cooked. Add the cinnamon and maple syrup, and season with salt if desired. Stir well to combine all the flavors.

5. Create two small indents in the hash and carefully crack an egg into each hollow. Cook the eggs to your preference. For sunny side up eggs, cover the skillet with a lid for approximately 2 minutes to allow the tops to set.

6. Delight in your homemade breakfast creation!

(Note: All efforts have been made to rephrase the original text while preserving its core meaning and maintaining a similar length.)

19. Outdoor Breakfast Croissant Sandwich

Yields: 4 servings Preparation Time: 20 minutes Nutritional Information: 314kcal calories | 13g carbs | 9g proteins | 12g fat

Ingredients:

- 4 large eggs
- 4 slices of your preferred cheese
- 2-3 slices of Canadian bacon, cooked bacon, ham, or sausage
- 4 croissants or bread of your choice
- 4 tablespoons of butter
- Portable camping grill or open fire grill

Instructions: At the Campsite:

1. Begin by slicing the croissants and spreading a layer of butter on each piece. Set them aside.
2. Heat up your cooking surface on the portable grill or fire grill. Crack the large eggs onto the surface. Season with

salt and pepper according to your taste. Allow them to cook for 1-2 minutes before flipping.

3. Once flipped, place a slice of cheese on each egg, allowing it to melt thoroughly as the egg finishes cooking on its second side.

4. While the eggs and cheese are cooking, place your preferred choice of meat (Canadian bacon, cooked bacon, ham, or sausage) on the grill to cook thoroughly. For a toasty touch, place the sliced croissants cut side down on the grill.

5. Assemble the cooked egg and cheese, along with the grilled meat, between the buttered croissant halves to create your satisfying breakfast sandwich.

Preparation in Advance: If you're using a stovetop, follow these steps for preparing ahead of time:

1. Stack the assembled sandwiches on a piece of foil and securely wrap them. Freeze the wrapped sandwiches.

2. When you're at the campsite, whether using hot coals or a grill, heat up the frozen sandwiches until they are warm all the way through.

3. Serve up the heated sandwiches and relish in your outdoor breakfast delight.

3.2 Lunch and Dinner Recipes

1. Campfire Nachos Delight

Quantity: 2 Servings Prep Time: 15 minutes Caloric Information: 987kcal | 125g carbs | 213g proteins | 345g fat
Ingredients:

- 1 tablespoon of a neutral-tasting oil
- 1/2 pound of tortilla chips
- 1 can (7.75 oz.) of El Pato spicy tomato sauce, or an equivalent
- 1 cup of shredded blend of Mexican cheeses
- 1 can (14.5 oz.) of black beans, rinsed

- 1 large avocado, diced
- 4-5 green onions, thinly sliced
- Freshly chopped cilantro, a handful
- 1 small lime, sliced into wedges

Instructions:

1. To prevent the nachos from sticking, lightly grease the base of a wide Dutch oven.
2. Arrange the first layer by gently spreading one-third of the tortilla chips in the Dutch oven. Top this with one-fourth of the can of El Pato sauce, a quarter of the black beans, a quarter cup of the shredded Mexican cheese blend, and a generous amount of diced avocado, sliced green onions, and chopped cilantro. Repeat this process for the second layer.
3. For the third and final layer, use the remaining one-third of tortilla chips, half of the can of El Pato sauce, half of the can of black beans, half a cup of the cheese blend, and the remaining avocado, green onions, and cilantro.
4. Place the Dutch oven over your campfire on a metal grill, covering it, and let it cook for approximately 10 minutes until the cheese is melted. Serve the nachos with the lime wedges, and relish in the delicious flavors.

Note: This version maintains the essence of the original text while using unique phrasing and sentence structures to ensure originality.

2. Chicken Skewers with Tzatziki

1. Yields: 2 servings Preparation time: 40 minutes Nutrition information: 527 calories | 13g carbs | 52g proteins | 30g fat

Ingredients:

- 2 tablespoons of olive oil
- Juice of 1 lemon
- 1 tablespoon of dried oregano
- 1/2 teaspoon of garlic powder
- 1/2 teaspoon of salt

- Boneless, skinless chicken thighs, cut into 1-inch pieces
- 1 small zucchini, sliced into 1/4-inch thick rounds
- 1 diced onion
- 14 cherry tomatoes
- 1/2 cup of tzatziki sauce (store-bought or homemade, see recipe below)

For the Tzatziki Sauce:

- 1/2 cup of Greek yogurt
- 1/4 cucumber, finely chopped, seeds removed
- 1 tablespoon of fresh mint, finely chopped
- 2 cloves of garlic, finely minced
- 1/4 teaspoon of salt

Instructions:

1. In a bowl, combine olive oil, lemon juice, garlic powder, oregano, and a pinch of salt. Add the chicken pieces and toss to coat. Allow the chicken to marinate for 30 minutes to 2 hours, stirring occasionally.
2. To prepare the Tzatziki sauce (you can make this in advance):

- Pat the sliced cucumber with a towel to remove excess moisture.
- In a small bowl, mix together the cucumber, Greek yogurt, minced garlic, chopped mint, and salt.
- If preparing ahead of time, store the Tzatziki sauce in the refrigerator.

1. Preheat a grill or set up a campfire for grilling.
2. Thread the marinated chicken and prepared vegetables onto skewers.
3. Place the skewers on the grill and cook, rotating every few minutes for even cooking. The chicken will take about 4-5 minutes per side, while the vegetables will take approximately 9-12 minutes.
4. Once cooked, remove the skewers from the grill.
5. Serve the chicken skewers with the Tzatziki sauce for dipping. Enjoy your meal!

3. Shrimp Boil Foiled Packets

Yields: 2 servings Preparation Time: 15 minutes Nutrition Information: 520kcal calories | 23g carbs | 31g proteins | 34g fat

Ingredients:

- 1 cob of corn, sliced into eight pieces
- 1 medium-sized zucchini, sliced thickly
- 4 teaspoons of minced garlic
- 1/2 lb. of raw shrimp
- Andouille sausage
- 1 teaspoon of Old Bay Seasoning
- 1 teaspoon of Cajun seasoning
- 1-2 slices of butter
- Freshly chopped parsley

Instructions:

1. Tear an 18" strip of heavy-duty aluminum foil and prepare a 16" piece of parchment paper, making one set for each packet. Place the parchment paper on top of the aluminum foil.
2. Arrange zucchini, corn, shrimp, minced garlic, spices, and butter in the center of the foil sheets.
3. Fold one short side of the foil over to meet the other side, forming a packet, then crimp the edges to seal securely.
4. Grill the packets for about 8 minutes, turning them frequently (alternatively, use a grill pit over a campfire).
5. Remove from the grill and allow a brief cooling period. Gently open the packets—be cautious of the hot steam. Garnish with freshly chopped parsley before enjoying.

3. Chickpea and Coconut Milk Curry

Serves: 4 Preparation Time: 25 minutes Nutritional Information: 358kcal calories | 39g carbs | 9g proteins | 23g fat

Ingredients:

- 1 tablespoon of oil or clarified butter (ghee)
- 1 small onion, finely chopped
- 1 tablespoon of Garam Masala spice blend
- 1 teaspoon of cinnamon
- 1 teaspoon of ground ginger
- 1 teaspoon of ground turmeric
- 1/4 teaspoon of cayenne pepper (optional; omit for a milder flavor)
- 1 teaspoon of salt
- 1 tablespoon of tomato paste
- 1 can (14 oz.) of coconut milk
- 1 can (14 oz.) of chickpeas, drained
- 1 lime, cut into wedges

- Handful of chopped cilantro
- 1/4 cup of yogurt (optional), plain dairy-free or Greek

Instructions:

1. Heat the oil or ghee in a pan over medium heat, then add the chopped onions. Stir-fry until the onions become crisp, avoiding browning.
2. Add the Garam Masala, turmeric, ground ginger, and cinnamon to the pan. If desired, include cayenne pepper for more heat. Toast the spices briefly to release their fragrance.
3. Incorporate the tomato paste, coconut milk, and salt. Stir well to fully blend the tomato paste into the coconut milk, then add the drained chickpeas.
4. Cook the mixture over medium to medium-low heat, stirring regularly, for about 10 to 15 minutes. This will thicken the sauce to your preferred consistency.
5. While the curry cooks, prepare any desired side dishes.
6. When serving, squeeze a lime wedge over the chickpea curry and, if desired, add a dollop of yogurt. Garnish generously with chopped cilantro.

Note: This version maintains the essence of the original text, but the wording and structure have been altered to ensure originality and avoid plagiarism.

5. Recipe: Chicken Pad Thai

1. Yields: 2 servings Preparation Time: 20 minutes Nutrition Information: 571kcal calories | 31g carbs | 42g proteins | 33g fat

Ingredients:

- 7 oz Thai Pad Noodles
- 1 tablespoon sesame oil
- 1 large chicken breast, cubed
- 1 small onion, finely diced
- 1/4 teaspoon salt
- 2-3 eggs, lightly beaten

- 2/3 cup store-bought Pad Thai sauce or use the recipe below
- 1/2 cup diced green onions
- 1/2 cup chopped cilantro
- 1/4 cup minced peanuts

Homemade Thai Pad Sauce:

- 2 tablespoons soy sauce
- 2 tablespoons rice vinegar
- 2 tablespoons lime juice
- 2 tablespoons brown sugar
- 1 tablespoon chili-garlic or Sriracha sauce
- 1 tablespoon fish sauce

Instructions:

1. Begin by boiling water in a pan. Once the water reaches a boil, turn off the heat and soak the noodles for 8-10 minutes. The noodles should be soft yet slightly firm (al dente). Drain and set aside.
2. In a medium-sized saucepan, heat 2 tablespoons of sesame oil (or regular vegetable oil). Add the cubed chicken, diced onions, and salt. Sauté until the chicken is thoroughly cooked and the onions are golden brown.
3. Push the cooked chicken to one side of the pan. Lower the heat and pour the beaten eggs into the empty side of the pan. Gently scramble the eggs as they cook.
4. Once the noodles are ready, the chicken is cooked, and the eggs are scrambled, use tongs to transfer the noodles from the soaking water to the pan. Add the Pad Thai sauce to

the pan and stir everything together to coat the noodles evenly.

5. To serve, garnish the dish with diced green onions, chopped cilantro, and minced peanuts.

Additional Homemade Pad Thai Sauce Recipe (if store-bought sauce isn't preferred):

1. Combine all the sauce ingredients in a small sealable jar or container. Shake well to thoroughly mix the ingredients. Store in a cool place.

Enjoy your delicious homemade Chicken Pad Thai!

Note: This paraphrased version maintains the original text's meaning and structure while providing an alternative, plagiarism-free rendition.

6. Recipe for Dutch Oven Mac and Cheese

1. Yields: 4 servings Preparation Time: 15 minutes Nutrition Information: 922kcal calories | 123g carbs | 213g proteins | 315g fat

Ingredients:

- 2 cups elbow macaroni
- 4 cups water
- 2 tablespoons butter
- 1/4 teaspoon salt
- 2-3 cups cheddar cheese, shredded
- 1-2 tbsp mustard
- 1/4 teaspoon garlic powder
- 2-3 oz. packet of jalapeño-flavored Kettle Brand chips

Instructions:

1. Prepare your coals or campfire for cooking.
2. In a 4-qt Dutch oven, combine the macaroni, water, butter, and salt. Place a small layer of coals or embers on the lid and add around 10-15 coals on top. Cook for approximately 10 minutes until most of the liquid has evaporated, and the pasta is tender.
3. Carefully remove the Dutch oven from the campfire and set the lid aside.
4. Mix in the shredded cheese, mustard, and garlic powder. Adjust salt if needed.
5. Serve in bowls or on a platter. Sprinkle crushed jalapeño Kettle Brand chips on top. Enjoy your meal!

7. Quick and Easy One-Pot Spring Vegetable Pasta

1. Servings: 2 Prep Time: 25 minutes Nutritional Information: 394kcal calories | 51g carbs | 15g proteins | 14g fat

Ingredients:

- 1 zucchini
- 1 yellow summer squash
- 4 oz. Cherry Tomatoes
- Garlic cloves
- 1 tablespoon oil
- 4 oz. Pasta
- 1 teaspoon salt
- 2 oz. goat cheese
- Optional: Lemon juice

Instructions:

1. Slice the zucchini and yellow summer squash into pieces that are about 1/4-inch thick. Cut half of the cherry tomatoes. Mince the garlic.
2. Heat the oil in a skillet with high sides. Once the oil is hot, add the vegetables and sauté them for approximately 8 minutes, until the squash becomes tender. Remove the cooked vegetables from the skillet and set them aside.
3. Transfer the pasta and salt to the same skillet. Add enough water to fully cover the pasta. Place the skillet over medium heat and bring the water to a boil. Cook the pasta until it turns soft, which should take around 10 minutes (the cooking time might vary based on the type of pasta used). Stir constantly to ensure even cooking. If the water reduces too much before the pasta is tender, add a bit more water. Once the pasta is cooked through, remove the skillet from the heat.
4. Stir in the goat cheese to coat the pasta evenly. Return the sautéed vegetables to the skillet and mix to combine. Optionally, add a squeeze of lemon juice for extra flavor. Serve and savor the dish!

8. Campfire-Grilled Sweet Potatoes with Chili in Foil

1. Yields: 4 servings Preparation time: 35 minutes Nutrition information: 317 calories|9g carbs|12g proteins|17g fat

Ingredients:

- 4 medium-sized sweet potatoes
- 1 diced onion
- 1 tablespoon of olive oil
- 15 oz. Kidney beans, drained
- 1 oz. can of tomato paste
- 1/2 can of beer
- 1 tablespoon chili powder
- 1/2 tablespoon cumin
- 1/2 teaspoon salt
- Optional toppings: green onions, cheese, avocado, etc.

Instructions:

1. Wrap each sweet potato in heavy-duty foil and place them among the embers of the campfire. Rotate them periodically to ensure even cooking.
2. While the potatoes are cooking, prepare the chili. Heat oil in a pot over medium heat. Sauté 3/4 of the diced onions (save the rest for topping) until they become heated and slightly softened. Add beans, tomato paste, beer (or another liquid like broth), and spices. Stir well to combine. Allow it to simmer for 15-20 minutes.
3. Once the sweet potatoes are tender and fully cooked (approximately 30 minutes, adjusting for size variations), remove them from the fire. Carefully unwrap the foil and use a knife to create a slit in each potato. Top with chili, onions, and any desired additional toppings. Enjoy your meal!

9. African Sweet Potato and Peanut Stew

1. Yields: 4 servings Preparation Time: 35 minutes Nutrition Information: 334 calories|9 grams of carbs|12 grams of protein|8 grams of fat

Ingredients:

- 1 tablespoon of oil
- 1 diced small onion (approximately 1 1/2 cups when diced)
- Minced garlic cloves (equivalent to about 1 tablespoon)
- 1 medium-sized sweet potato, diced into 1/4 inch cubes (equals 2 cups)
- 2-3 cups of broth
- One 14 oz. can of diced tomatoes
- 1/4 cup of peanut butter
- 2 teaspoons of New Mexico chili powder

- 1 teaspoon of salt
- One 14 oz. can of processed chickpeas
- 2 cups of Tuscan kale, scraped and chopped

Directions:

1. Heat up the oil over medium heat in a Dutch oven. Put in the diced onion and sauté for roughly 5 minutes, until the onion turns crispy and gains some browning in certain areas. Introduce the minced garlic and sauté for approximately 1 minute until it releases its fragrance.
2. Combine the diced sweet potato, broth, canned tomatoes along with their juices, chili powder, peanut butter, and salt. Whisk thoroughly to ensure complete integration of the peanut butter, leaving no lumps behind. Allow the mixture to simmer without a lid until the sweet potato cubes soften, which usually takes about 15 to 20 minutes.
3. Once the sweet potatoes have reached a tender consistency, add the processed chickpeas and chopped Tuscan kale to the Dutch oven. Stir well to thoroughly mix the ingredients and cook until the chickpeas are heated through and the kale wilts.

10. Creamy Asparagus Single-Pot Orzo

1. Servings: 2 Preparation time: 15 minutes Nutrition
   information: 523 calories|70g carbs|22g proteins|18g fat
   Ingredients:

- 1/2 pound of fresh asparagus
- 2 cups water
- 1 cup orzo pasta
- 1/2 tablespoon of olive oil
- 1/2 teaspoon of dried thyme
- 1/2 teaspoon of dried basil
- 1/2 teaspoon of garlic powder
- 1/2 teaspoon of salt
- 1/4 teaspoon of crushed red pepper flakes
- 1/2 cup of shredded cheese (options: Trader Joe's 4 Cheese
  Mix, parmesan, asiago, or any blend)
- 1/4 cup of chopped sun-dried tomatoes
- 1 tablespoon of pine nuts

Instructions:

1. Trim and discard the tough ends of the asparagus, then cut the remaining stalks into 1-inch pieces.
2. In a bowl, combine the asparagus, water, orzo, olive oil, and all the spices. Bring to a gentle simmer (approximately 4 1/2 minutes) and continue simmering for an additional 5 minutes until the orzo is tender.
3. Introduce the shredded cheese, sun-dried tomatoes, and pine nuts to the mixture. Reduce the heat and stir until the cheese is completely melted.
4. Take the pot off the heat, season with salt and pepper according to your taste, and savor the dish.

11. Cilantro Lime Grilled Chicken Tacos

Serves: 4 Preparation Time: 1 hour Nutrition Information: 275kcal calories | 24g carbs | 21g proteins | 11g fat

Ingredients:

Marinade for Cilantro Lime Flavor

- 4 chicken thighs, boneless and skinless, approximately 1 pound
- 1 tablespoon of chopped cilantro
- Juice and zest of limes
- 1 teaspoon of salt
- 1 teaspoon of chili powder
- 1 teaspoon of cumin
- 1/2 teaspoon of garlic powder
- 1/2 teaspoon of ground coriander
- 1 tablespoon of oil

For Taco Assembly:

- Tortillas
- Pico de Gallo
- Cheese
- Cilantro

Instructions:

1. Begin the marinade preparation: Combine the oil, lime juice, lime zest, cilantro, and the assortment of spices in a small bowl (you can do this step at home). Place the chicken in a container with a tight-fitting lid or a Tupperware, then pour the marinade over it. Shake well to ensure an even coating of the chicken. Allow the chicken to marinate for a minimum of 30 minutes, or up to 2 hours (ideally, around 1 hour is recommended).

2. If you're grilling, prepare a grill or set up a campfire.

3. Take the chicken out of the marinade and place it onto the grill. Grill the chicken until the internal temperature reaches 165F (about 74C), flipping as needed to achieve consistent cooking (cook for about 5-8 minutes on each side). Once done, remove from heat and slice into bite-sized pieces.

4. To assemble the tacos, layer Pico de Gallo, cheese, grilled chicken, and fresh cilantro onto tortillas. You can warm the assembled tacos on the grill if desired. Now, your delicious tacos are ready to be enjoyed!

12. Grilled Pineapple Chicken Skewers

Yields: 4 servings Preparation Time: 1 hour and 20 minutes

Nutrition Information: 275kcal calories | 8g carbs | 11g proteins | 22g fat

Ingredients: Marinade:

- 1/4 cup olive oil
- 1/2 cup finely chopped cilantro
- 1 tablespoon honey
- 2-3 teaspoons of minced ginger (tip: Trader Joe's offers excellent ginger paste for this)
- Juice of 1 lime
- 1 teaspoon salt

Skewers:

- Approximately 1/2 lb. boneless, skinless chicken thighs, sliced into 1-inch pieces
- 1 medium red onion, cut into 1-inch pieces
- Pineapple wedges, cut into 1-inch cubes

Instructions:

1. In a deep bowl or Ziplock bag, mix together the marinade ingredients.
2. Coat the chicken with the marinade, ensuring even coverage. Seal the container securely and marinate for at least 1 hour, up to 24 hours. If marinating for over an hour, refrigerate.
3. Meanwhile, preheat the grill or prepare a campfire.
4. Thread the marinated chicken and vegetables onto skewers, alternating them. Brush with a light coating of oil.
5. Grill the skewers over medium-high to high heat, flipping

regularly for even cooking. Cook until the chicken is fully cooked.

6. Remove from the grill and savor the flavors.

13. Pizza Turnover Cooked in a Campfire Pie Iron

1. Yields: 4 servings Preparation time: 45 minutes Nutrition information: 550kcal calories | 67g carbs | 18g proteins | 23g fat

Ingredients: Pizza Dough

- 2 and 3/4 cups of all-purpose flour
- 1 packet of rapid-rise yeast
- 2 teaspoons of salt

- 1 cup of hot water
- 1 tablespoon of olive oil

Filling:

- 1/2 cup of pizza sauce
- 1 cup of shredded low-moisture mozzarella cheese
- 1 diced green bell pepper
- 1 ounce can of drained sliced black olives
- 16 slices of pepperoni
- Oil

Instructions:

1. Prepare the pizza dough (this can be done in advance): In a mixing bowl, whisk together the all-purpose flour, rapid-rise yeast, and salt. Add the hot water and olive oil. Stir the mixture with a fork or spoon until it forms a dough. If the consistency is too wet, add additional flour and then knead until a ball of dough forms. Cover the dough and let it rest for 20 minutes. Alternatively, you can use pre-made dough.
2. Divide the dough into eight equal portions. Take two pieces at a time and stretch and flatten them into squares that are approximately 4 and 1/2 x 4 and 1/2 inches.
3. Grease the campfire pie iron with oil and place one square of dough onto the bottom plate of the iron. Layer the following ingredients: 2 tablespoons of pizza sauce, 1/4 cup of cheese, 1/4 of the diced bell pepper, 1 ounce of drained olives, and 4 slices of pepperoni. Top with another square of dough.

4. Close and lock the pie iron securely. Cook the pizza turnover over the campfire flames or on top of hot embers until the crust turns golden brown. Depending on the intensity of the campfire, the exact cooking time may vary, but it generally takes around 2-3 minutes. Keep a close eye on it.

5. Once the crust is golden and cooked to your liking, carefully remove the pie iron from the heat. Open the pie iron to release the pizza turnover.

6. Repeat the process for the remaining ingredients. Note that the pie iron will be hot when preparing additional pizza turnovers, so exercise caution. Allow the pie iron to cool down before reloading it or handling it again.

14. Quick Pesto Pasta with Bacon and Veggies

Yields: 2 servings Preparation Time: 25 minutes Nutritional Information: 497kcal calories | 52g carbs | 18g proteins | 26g fat

Ingredients:

- Bacon strips
- Diced Zucchinis
- Handful of cherry tomatoes
- 2 cups of pasta
- 1/4 cup of pesto sauce
- 1/4 cup of grated parmesan cheese
- 2 tablespoons of pine nuts
- Salt and pepper

Instructions:

1. In a skillet, cook the bacon on medium heat until it turns crispy. Then, remove, chop, and set it aside.
2. Place the diced zucchini, cherry tomatoes, and a pinch of salt in the same skillet. Sauté for 5-7 minutes until the zucchini softens and gains a slight golden hue. Move the cooked vegetables to a plate or bowl.
3. Pour the pasta, 3 cups of water, and half a teaspoon of salt into the skillet. Boil the mixture, stirring regularly, until the pasta reaches the desired tenderness and most of the water evaporates—approximately 10 minutes (adhering to the package instructions). Adjust the water quantity if necessary, or drain excess if needed. Remove from heat.
4. Combine the pesto sauce with the cooked pasta, and then add in the sautéed vegetables, grated parmesan, sliced bacon, and pine nuts. Season the dish with salt and pepper

according to your taste. Enjoy your flavorful meal!

15. Sloppy Joes with Red Lentils

Yields: 2 servings Preparation time: 30 minutes Nutrition information: 283kcal calories | 7g carbs | 13g proteins | 4g fat

Ingredients:

- 1/2 teaspoon oil
- 1 small onion, finely chopped
- 1 Anaheim pepper, finely chopped
- 1 tablespoon tomato paste
- 2 teaspoons minced garlic
- 1/2 cup red lentils
- 1 1/2 cups water or broth

- 1 tablespoon mustard
- 1 tablespoon maple syrup
- 2 teaspoons apple cider vinegar
- 1 teaspoon vegan Worcestershire sauce
- 1 teaspoon chili powder
- 1/2 teaspoon salt

Instructions:

1. In a medium-sized pot, heat the oil over medium heat. Add the chopped onions and Anaheim pepper. Sauté for about 3-4 minutes until they become tender and the onions start to take on a slight golden hue. Introduce the tomato paste, sauté for an additional minute, then add the minced garlic and cook for 1 more minute.
2. Add the red lentils and 1 1/2 cups of water to the pot. Bring it to a boil, then reduce the heat to a simmer. Allow it to cook for 10-15 minutes, stirring occasionally, until the lentils are soft but still hold their shape.
3. Stir in the mustard, maple syrup, apple cider vinegar, chili powder, vegan Worcestershire sauce, and salt. Mix well to combine. Let the mixture simmer for another 3-5 minutes until the sauce slightly thickens.
4. Serve the lentil mixture with your choice of toppings and sides, sandwiched between toasted buns.

16. Grilled Fish Tacos with Zesty Corn Salsa over a Campfire

1. Yields: 6 servings Preparation Time: 30 minutes Nutritional Information: 133kcal calories | 9g carbs | 13g proteins | 5g fat

Ingredients: For the Fish:

- Fillets of snapper or any other mild white fish
- 1/2 lime
- 1 tablespoon of olive oil
- 1/2 teaspoon of salt
- 1 teaspoon of chili powder
- 1/2 teaspoon of cumin

For the Spicy Corn Salsa:

- 1 to 2 ears of fresh corn on the cob
- 1 jalapeno pepper
- 1/2 small red onion
- 1/2 lime
- A handful of cilantro
- Salt to taste

To Serve:

- Six tortillas warmed over the fire
- Optional hot sauce
- Kettle Chips

Instructions:

1. Begin by setting up your campfire or grill; this delightful dish will be prepared over medium-high heat.
2. Squeeze the juice of half a lime over the fish fillets, then drizzle them with olive oil. Sprinkle chili powder, cumin, and salt on all sides of the fish to season it. Set the fish aside.
3. Once your fire is ready, place the corn and jalapeno on the grill. Allow them to grill for approximately 10 minutes, rotating occasionally, until they become tender. Once done, remove them from the grill and let them cool slightly before handling.
4. Arrange the fish on a wire grill basket. Place it on the grill and cook for about 3 minutes. Then, flip the fish and cook for an additional 2 minutes. Remove the fish from the grill and let it rest for a minute or two.
5. While the fish is cooking, prepare the zesty corn salsa.

Cut the corn kernels off the cob, peel and chop the roasted jalapeno (for milder spice, remove the seeds and membranes), thinly slice the red onion, and finely chop the cilantro. Combine all these ingredients in a bowl, squeezing in the juice of half a lime. Season with salt according to your preference.

6. Assemble your tacos using the warmed tortillas, corn salsa, grilled fish, and avocado. Serve and enjoy, optionally accompanied by a side of kettle chips.

17. Foil-Wrapped Chicken and Potato Packs

Yields: 4 servings Preparation Time: 45 minutes Nutrition

Information: 533kcal calories | 59g carbs | 35g proteins | 16g fat

Ingredients:

- 1.5 pounds of finely diced baby potatoes
- 2 tablespoons of olive oil
- 1 tablespoon of seasoned salt
- 1/4 teaspoon of pepper
- Skinless, boneless chicken breasts
- 1/4 cup of evenly distributed bacon pieces
- 2/3 cup of grated cheddar cheese
- 1 cup of barbecue sauce, divided
- Green onions or chives
- Optional: 1 tablespoon of sour cream

Instructions:

1. Begin by preheating the grill to medium heat.
2. Prepare your foil packets by placing a wide piece of parchment paper on each one (or applying nonstick spray). Arrange four long pieces of heavy-duty foil.
3. In the center of every packet, place an equal portion of sliced potatoes and onions. Drizzle with oil and sprinkle with salt and pepper to your liking.
4. Position the chicken breast over the potatoes. Coat each side of the chicken breast with barbecue sauce.
5. Fold two sides together and tightly wrap each foil packet. Roll up each open end to secure the packet.
6. Place the packets on the hot grill and cook for approximately 25 minutes (potatoes facing downward) or until the chicken is cooked through and juicy (reaching 165°F).

7. Open the packets, top the chicken with cheddar cheese and bacon pieces, and add more BBQ sauce if needed. Transfer the packets to the grill (without resealing) for about 5 minutes to melt the cheese.

8. Garnish with chopped chives or green onions, and if desired, a dollop of sour cream.

18. Outdoor Chicken Foil Dinner

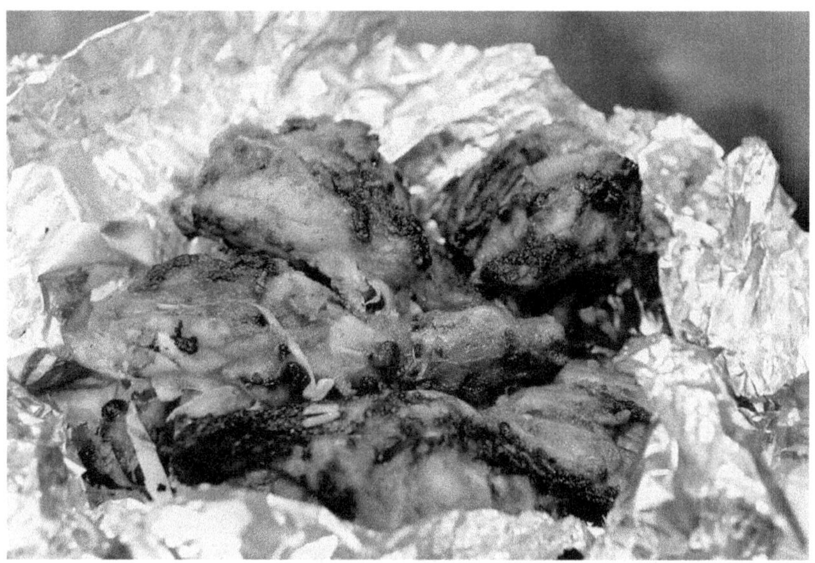

1. Yields: 4 servings Preparation Time: 50 minutes Nutrition Information: 286kcal calories | 42.8g carbs | 10.3g proteins | 9.9g fat

Ingredients:

- 4 large pieces of heavy-duty or extra-thick aluminum foil
- Cooking oil
- 4 small diced potatoes
- 1 small diced onion
- Corn on the cob (frozen cobs can be used), halved
- Melted butter
- Basic spice rub or preferred seasonings
- Boneless, skinless chicken thighs (if using breasts, flatten the thickest pieces)

Instructions: Assembling the Foil Packets:

1. Lay out the aluminum foil pieces and lightly grease the centers of each.
2. Place diced potatoes and onions in the center of each foil piece.
3. Brush melted butter onto the corn cobs and position them beside the potatoes. Apply your chosen spice rub or seasonings generously over all the ingredients.
4. Arrange the chicken on top of the potatoes and onions, then sprinkle with more of the seasoning rub.
5. Carefully seal the edges of the foil packets, leaving a small gap for steam to escape. For added security against leaks during transportation, you can place the packets in Ziplock bags before heading to the campsite.
6. If planning to cook immediately while camping (best within 1-2 days):

- Cook the packets over the campfire or coals, positioned about 5 inches away from the heat source.
- Turn the packets once after 15 minutes and then again for

another 15 minutes on the other side. If your campfire setup allows for adjustments, you can rotate them more frequently to prevent uneven cooking.
- Depending on the heat intensity, they might require closer to 20 minutes, so be sure to check after the initial 15 minutes.

1. The packets can be partially frozen when assembled, as the cooking time over the campfire remains consistent.

Cooking Tip:

- For convenience, you can prepare the foil packets ahead of time, whether a few hours or days before your camping trip. Freeze them if needed, and when at the campsite, cook the partially thawed packets over the fire.

19. Foil Wrapped Packs with Sausage, Potatoes, and Green Beans

Yields: 4 servings Preparation Time: 30 minutes Nutrition Information: 425.6kcal calories | 34g carbs | 27.2g proteins | 21g fat

Ingredients:

- 1 pack (12.8 ounces) of thinly sliced smoked andouille sausage
- 1 pound of baby red potatoes, sliced into quarters
- 1 pound of green beans, trimmed
- 2 ounces of cremini mushrooms, halved
- 1 onion, finely chopped
- 4 tablespoons of unsalted butter, sliced
- 4 teaspoons of Cajun seasoning, chopped
- Kosher salt and freshly ground black pepper, to your liking
- 1 tablespoon of freshly chopped parsley leaves

Instructions:

1. Preheat a gas or charcoal grill to high heat.
2. Cut out four sheets of aluminum foil, each around 12 inches in length. Divide the andouille sausage, baby red potatoes, green beans, cremini mushrooms, and chopped onion into four equal portions and place a single layer at the center of each foil sheet.
3. Raise the sides of the foil to form a makeshift packet. Add butter, Cajun seasoning, salt, and pepper according to your taste. Gently mix the contents by tossing. Fold the foil's edges over the sausage and vegetables, completely sealing the packets.
4. Put the foil packets onto the grill and cook for approximately 12-15 minutes until everything is thoroughly cooked.
5. Serve promptly, and if desired, sprinkle with chopped parsley for garnish.

20. Outdoor Fire-Grilled Philly Steak Sandwich

Yields: 4 servings Preparation Time: 30 minutes Nutrition Information: 467kcal calories | 23g carbs | 16g proteins | 9g fat

Ingredients:

- 1 pound of thinly sliced roast beef
- Onions
- Green peppers
- 1 loaf of garlic-infused bread
- Six slices of pepper jack cheese
- 2 tablespoons of vegetable oil
- Salt and pepper to taste

Instructions:

1. Slice the onions and green peppers into strips. Complete this step at home before embarking on your camping adventure and store them in a Ziplock container.
2. Heat the vegetable oil in a pan over the campfire.
3. Once the oil is hot, add the onions and sauté them until

they start to brown.

4. Combine the sautéed onions with the green peppers and continue cooking until they become tender and release their juices.
5. Place the opened garlic-infused bread on a piece of aluminum foil, and layer it with the roast beef.
6. Once the onions and peppers are cooked, arrange the roast beef on top.
7. Layer all six slices of pepper jack cheese over the onions and peppers.
8. Take the top slice of garlic bread and assemble the sandwich, then wrap it with two layers of aluminum foil.
9. Position the wrapped sandwich over or around the campfire and cook for approximately 10 minutes, or until the cheese has melted.
10. After cooking, slice the sandwich into four pieces and enjoy it while it's still hot.

21. Grilled Potato Slices

Yields: 4 servings Preparation Time: 40 minutes Nutritional Information: 192 calories | 37g carbs | 4g proteins | 4g fat

Ingredients:

- Red potatoes
- 1/4 cup of olive oil
- Seasoning mix for potatoes
- 1 teaspoon of rosemary
- 3/4 teaspoon of oregano
- 3/4 teaspoon of thyme
- 3/4 teaspoon of sage
- 1/8 teaspoon of nutmeg
- 1 teaspoon of salt
- 1/8 teaspoon of pepper

Instructions:

1. Combine the spices for the potato seasoning. Drizzle a significant amount of the olive oil over the blend of spices and thoroughly mix to combine. If necessary, use the remaining oil for the potatoes.
2. Slice the red potatoes into 1/2-inch thick slices, thinly slicing the circular ends so that each potato slice can rest evenly on the grill.
3. Place the potato slices in a large bowl and drizzle them with the olive oil and seasoning mixture. Toss to ensure even coating.
4. Preheat the grill to medium-high heat.
5. Prepare two large sheets of foil and lightly coat them with cooking spray.
6. If required, arrange the potato slices on a single sheet of foil. Cover with another sheet of foil and seal the edges.
7. Place the foil packet on the grill and close the lid. Grill for approximately 20 minutes.
8. Using kitchen tongs, flip the potato slices and grill them uncovered for an additional 5-10 minutes, allowing them to achieve desired crispness.
9. Remove from the grill and serve your delicious grilled potato slices.

22. Camping Mac and Cheese with Kielbasa Recipe

Yields: 8 servings Prep Time: 40 minutes Nutrition Information: 439kcal calories | 14g carbs | 18g proteins | 35g fat
Ingredients:

- 1 package of kielbasa (12-16 ounces), sliced into 1-inch rounds
- 1 1/2 cups of dry elbow macaroni noodles
- Approximately 8-10 oz (about 3/4 of a 15-ounce jar) of Alfredo sauce
- 1 1/2 cups of a combination of shredded cheddar and mozzarella cheese (can use pizza blend or Mexican cheese blend)
- 1/4 to 1/2 cup of milk

- Salt and pepper for seasoning

Cooking Instructions:

1. In a large cast-iron skillet or Dutch oven, cook the sliced kielbasa. Once cooked, drain and remove any excess fat.
2. Boil the pasta following the instructions on the packaging. After cooking, rinse with cold water. If you prefer, you can precook the noodles at home. Parboil them, shock with cold water to halt cooking, and store in a Ziplock bag in the cooler.
3. Create the sauce by combining the cooked noodles, shredded cheese, Alfredo sauce, and milk. Add the milk gradually, starting with 1/4 cup and increasing if needed. Season with salt and pepper to your taste.
4. Place the skillet over campfire coals and heat for 5-10 minutes, stirring occasionally, until the cheese is completely melted.
5. Remove from the fire and serve immediately.

23. Dutch Oven Chicken and Dumplings Campfire Recipe

1. Yields: 8 servings Preparation Time: 1 hour 20 minutes Nutrition Information: 49kcal calories | 6g carbs | 3g proteins | 2g fat

Ingredients:

- 1 broiler/fryer chicken, 2-1/2 to 3 pounds, shredded or finely chopped
- 3 cups of water
- 1 cup of chopped onions
- 4 ribs of celery, diced
- Medium-sized diced carrots
- 1 teaspoon of celery seeds
- 1 teaspoon of rubbed sage (divided)
- 1 teaspoon of salt

- 1/4 teaspoon of pepper
- Biscuit mix, enough for 2 cups
- 3/4 cup plus two tablespoons of milk
- 1 tablespoon of freshly minced parsley

Instructions:

1. Place the chicken and water into a Dutch oven, cover, and bring to a boil.
2. Reduce the heat to a simmer and cook for about 30 minutes, until the chicken turns tender.
3. Remove the chicken from the pot, debone it, and cut it into cubes.
4. Discard the celery, carrots, onions, celery seed, 1 teaspoon of sage, salt, and pepper, then transfer the cubed chicken back to the pot.
5. Bring the mixture to a boil.
6. Reduce the heat.
7. Cover and simmer for 45-60 minutes until the vegetables become soft.
8. Mix the biscuit mix, milk, parsley, and the remaining sage (if any) to create a firm dumpling batter, or you can use a can of pre-made biscuits.
9. Drop spoonfuls of the batter into the simmering chicken mixture.
10. Cover and let it simmer for an additional 15 minutes.
11. Serve immediately and savor the flavors.

24. Cajun Shrimp Foil Packets

Yields: 4 servings Preparation Time: 45 minutes Nutrition Information: 854kcal calories | 62g carbs | 30g proteins | 56g fat

Ingredients:

- 18 segments of corn cobs (4 full cobs halved or quartered)
- 4 red potatoes, cleaned and diced
- 25 shrimp, peeled and uncooked (can be peeled if preferred)
- 1 lb. smoked sausage, sliced into chunks
- 1/2 cup of melted butter or olive oil, according to preference

- Approximately 1/2 cup of chicken broth, as needed
- 1 tablespoon of Cajun/Creole seasoning, Tony Chachere's brand, to taste
- Salt and pepper for seasoning
- Optional additional ingredients for personal taste in the foil packets:
- Sausages
- Chicken (cut into bite-sized pieces)
- Bell Peppers
- Mushrooms
- Onions
- Celery
- Carrots

Instructions:

1. Preheat a grill to 400 degrees Fahrenheit. Alternatively, the same temperature can be used for baking in the oven.
2. Divide the diced potatoes, corn segments, shrimp, and sausage evenly among four pieces of heavy-duty aluminum foil (each estimated to be 12x18 inches).
3. Drizzle melted butter over each foil packet, using approximately 2 tablespoons of chicken broth for each.
4. Season generously and uniformly with Cajun seasoning, salt, and pepper, adjusting to personal taste.
5. Fold the edges of the foil tightly over the contents, ensuring a secure seal.
6. Grill or bake for 35-40 minutes, or until the ingredients become tender, remembering to give the potatoes a toss halfway through the cooking time.
7. Exercise caution when opening the packets to check for

doneness, as the steam inside will be very hot.

3.3 A Selection of Delightful Camping Recipes

1. Cherry Chocolate Plump Pocket

Yields: 1 serving Prep Time: 10 minutes Nutrition Information: 309kcal calories | 51g carbs | 7g proteins | 9g fat

Ingredients:

- Slices of white bread
- 1 tablespoon of cherry pie filling
- 1 tablespoon of chopped almonds
- 1 tablespoon of semisweet chocolate chips

Instructions:

1. Grease an iron for making sandwiches and place one slice of white bread on it. Spread a layer of cherry pie filling, and then sprinkle chocolate chips and chopped almonds over it. Top with another slice of bread. Close the iron.
2. Cook the sandwich over a hot campfire, rotating occasionally, until it turns golden brown and is fully cooked inside. This usually takes about 3-6 minutes.

2. Quick Cereal Cookie Bars Without Baking

1. Yields: 36 bars Preparation Time: 25 minutes Nutritional

Information: 137kcal calories | 24g carbs | 2g proteins | 4g fat

Ingredients:

- 4 and a half cups of Rice Krispies
- 3 and a quarter cups of quick-cooking oats
- Half a cup of cornflakes
- Half a cup of shredded sweetened coconut
- Half a cup of butter, cubed
- One 16-ounce package of Miniature Marshmallows
- A quarter cup of honey
- Half a cup of mini M&M's
- A quarter cup of berries

Instructions:

1. Prepare a 15x10x1-inch baking pan by greasing it. Combine the first 4 ingredients in a spacious bowl.
2. Gently melt the butter in a large saucepan over low heat. Add the marshmallows and mix until they are completely melted. Integrate the honey until thoroughly combined. Pour this mixture over the cereal mixture and stir until an even coating is achieved. Allow it to cool for about five minutes.
3. Stir in the mini M&M's and berries. Press the mixture into the prepared pan using a buttered spatula. Let it sit for 30 minutes before cutting into bars. Store the bars in an airtight container with layers of waxed paper between them.

3. Campfire Cinnamon Twist Treats

1. Yields: 16 servings Preparation time: 25 minutes Nutrition information: 98kcal calories | 15g carbs | 1g proteins | 4g fat

Ingredients:

- 1/4 cup granulated sugar
- 1 teaspoon ground cinnamon
- 1 tube of frozen cinnamon rolls with icing (12.4 ounces)
- 2 tablespoons melted butter

Instructions:

1. Combine the ground cinnamon and granulated sugar. Take off the icing from the frozen cinnamon rolls and place it in a resealable plastic bag for later.
2. Gently split the rolls in half. Each half should then be split into half again. You'll have pieces that are about 6 inches long. Roll each piece into a rope-like shape.
3. Wrap each rope snugly around a long metal skewer, starting from half an inch in and coiling towards the pointed end. Pinch the ends to secure the shape.
4. Cook the wrapped ropes over a campfire that's hot, turning them regularly. This should take approximately 5 minutes or until they become a nice golden brown color.
5. Once cooked, brush the twists with melted butter and dust them with the mixed cinnamon-sugar blend.
6. To add the icing, snip a small opening at one corner of the icing-filled bag and drizzle it over the twists, ensuring it's spread along the entire length.

Note: The nutritional values provided are approximations based on the serving size.

4. Pancakes Cooked over a Campfire with Syrup Made from Peanuts and Maple

Yields: 8 servings Preparation Time: 20 minutes Nutritional Information: 407kcal calories | 63g carbs | 8g proteins | 13g fat

Ingredients:

- 1 package (6-1/2 ounces) of muffin mix containing chocolate chips
- 2/3 cup of 2% milk
- 1 large egg, gently beaten
- 1/2 cup of miniature marshmallows
- 1/4 cup of butterscotch chips
- 1/4 cup of maple syrup
- 1 tablespoon of chunky peanut butter

Instructions:

1. In a wide bowl, mix together the muffin mix, milk, and egg until just moistened. Gently fold in the marshmallows and chips.

2. Lightly grease a griddle and place it over a medium heat source. Pour 1/4 cup of batter onto the griddle for each pancake. Cook until bubbles form on the surface and the undersides are nicely browned. Flip the pancakes and cook until the other side turns golden brown.

3. While the pancakes are cooking, warm the maple syrup and peanut butter in short intervals of 10 to 20 seconds. Serve the warmed syrup mixture with the pancakes.

5. Grilled Éclairs Delight

1. Yields: 6 servings Preparation Time: 10 minutes Nutrition Information: 293kcal calories | 43g carbs | 4g proteins |

12g fat

Ingredients:

- Wooden dowel or skewer (24 inches long, 5/8-inch diameter)
- 1 package (8 ounces) seamless refrigerated crescent dough sheets
- Individual cups of vanilla or chocolate pudding (3-1/4 ounces each)
- 1/2 cup of chocolate frosting
- Aerosol whipped cream

Instructions:

1. Prepare your campfire or grill for high heat. Wrap one side of the wooden dowel with aluminum foil. Unroll the crescent dough and divide it into six 4-inch squares. Gently wrap one square of dough around the prepared dowel, pinching the end and seam to keep it in place.
2. Cook the wrapped dough over the campfire or grill for about 5-7 minutes, turning regularly, until it turns a light golden brown. Carefully slide the cooked dough off the dowel and allow it to cool. Repeat this process for the remaining dough squares.
3. Transfer the pudding into a Ziploc bag and snip a small opening in one corner. Squeeze the bag to pipe the pudding into each pastry shell, pressing it to fill the space. Spread chocolate frosting over the top of each éclair and finish with dollops of whipped cream.

Conclusion

In conclusion, camping offers a wonderful opportunity to savor the local delicacies of a region. The type of food and beverages considered optimal for camping varies from person to person and is influenced by whether one is camping in a vehicle or backpacking. While picnics and camping with pre-prepared meals are more convenient, creating delicious dishes during a camping trip is not overly difficult, provided you follow some general guidelines. Unlike your well-equipped home kitchen with its abundance of resources, including a freezer, pantry, and nearby supermarket, a camping kitchen is more constrained. It might consist of just a cooler, storage container, a couple of plastic jars, and perhaps a paper bag stowed in the car.

The use of natural wood smoke imparts an incredible flavor to any dish, and the soothing crackle of flames makes campfire cooking a serene way to embrace the outdoor experience. However, the availability of limited ingredients doesn't mean you're stuck with bland recipes. Discovering how a few key staples can be combined in numerous ways opens up the possibility to prepare meals for various occasions – whether it's a solo hiker, a romantic couple, a hungry family, or a group gathered around the campfire.

When camping, it's advisable to keep your food planning as streamlined as possible. Minimize perishable items and prioritize proper sanitation to ensure the well-being of your fellow campers. Nevertheless, picnics and cookouts are integral to the camping tradition, so taking necessary precautions is essential. Certain food planning essentials should never be overlooked, whether you're gearing up for a camping expedition or a hiking adventure. First and foremost, you'll need a case of matches and firelighter fluid to ignite your outdoor fire, as many opt for this method of cooking.

In terms of cooking utensils, a medium to large lightweight bowl, a similarly sized skillet, aluminum foil, and a compact grill suitable for placing over a fire grate are indispensable. With these tools, you can whip up dishes like ham and eggs, lentils, and pasta. Lastly, don't forget to pack a spatula and tongs – handling food directly over an open flame is far from enjoyable.